STOCK MARKET INVESTING FOR BEGINNERS:

A 7 Day Crash Course to Learn How NOT to Lose Money and Ready-to-Use Simple Strategies to Achieve Financial Freedom Today!
(Options – Swing Trading)

BY

Bob Lee

Table of Contents

INTRODUCTION 3

PROS AND CONS OF STOCK MARKET INVESTING....25

THE MOST IMPORTANT THING: YOUR MINDSET 36

RISK AND MONEY MANAGEMENT 69

INVESTING STRATEGIES 94

EXCHANGE TRADED FUND 107

CONCLUSION..122

INTRODUCTION

This crash course is designed to teach potential traders and investors the rubrics, strategies, and dynamics of the stock market. During the course, you will be introduced to the fundamental aspects of the stock market and also given details on how the investment works. In the first section, you will be given information on areas such as; the stock market, stocks, history of finance, language of investing, types of investing among several others. This foundation will help prepare you for further and in-depth studies as we go through the course.

What is the Stock Market?

The stock market is also known as equity or share market. It is the aggregation of buyers and sellers of stocks, which represents an ownership claim on businesses. Stocks are also called shares. The stock of a corporation is all of the shares into which ownership of the corporation is divided. A single share of the stock represents fractional ownership of the corporation in proportion to the total number of shares. This typically entitles the stockholder to that fraction of the company's earnings, proceeds from the liquidation of assets after the discharge of all senior claims such as secured and unsecured debt, or voting power. This is often divided in proportion to the amount of money each stockholder has invested. Stocks are not necessarily equal; this is because certain classes of stock may be issued. For example, without voting rights, with enhanced voting rights, or with a certain priority to receive profits or liquidation proceeds before or after other classes of shareholders. Stocks can be bought and sold privately or on stock exchanges. The buying and selling processes are heavily regulated by governments to prevent fraud, protect investors, and benefit the larger economy. As a company issues new shares, the ownership and rights of existing shareholders are diluted in return for cash to sustain or grow the business. Companies can also buy back stock, which often lets investors recoup the initial investment plus capital gains from subsequent rises in stock price. Stock options, issued by many companies as part of employee compensation, do not represent ownership but represent the right to buy ownership at a future time at a specified price. This would represent a windfall to the employees if the option is exercised when the market price is higher than the promised price since if they immediately sold the stock, they would keep the difference (minus taxes). The owners of a private company may want additional capital to invest in new projects within the company. They may also simply wish to reduce their holding, freeing up capital for their own private use. They can achieve these goals by selling shares in the company to the general public, through a sale on a stock exchange. This process is called an initial public offering, or IPO. By selling shares, they can sell part or all of the company to many part-owners. The purchase of one share entitles the owner of that share to literally share in the ownership of the company, a fraction of the decision making power, and potentially a fraction of the profits, which the company may issue as dividends. The owner may also inherit debt and even litigation.

In the typical case of a publicly-traded firm, where there may be thousands of shareholders, it is impractical to have all of them making the daily decisions required to run a company. Thus, the shareholders will use their shares as votes in the election of members of the board of directors of the company. In a typical case, each share constitutes one vote. Corporations may, however, issue different classes of shares, which may have different voting rights. Owning the majority of the shares allows other shareholders to be out-voted effective control rests with the majority shareholder (or shareholders acting in concert). In this way, the original owners of the company often still have control of the company.

FREQUENTLY ASKED QUESTIONS ON STOCK MARKET

1. **Why do people buy stocks?**
2. **Why do companies issue stock?**
3. **What kinds of stock are there?**
4. **What are the benefits and risks of stocks?**
5. **How to buy and sell stocks**
6. **Understanding fees**
7. **Avoiding fraud**
8. **Shares**
9. **Shareholders rights**
10. **Stock Exchange**

Why do people buy stocks?

Investors buy stocks for various reasons. Here are some of them:

- Capital appreciation: This occurs when a stock rises in price.
- Dividend payments: This happens when the company distributes some of its earnings to stockholders.
- Ability to vote shares and influence the company.

Why do companies issue stock?

Companies issue stock to get money for various things, which may include:

- Paying off debt
- Launching new products
- Expanding into new markets or regions
- Enlarging facilities or building new ones

What kinds of stocks are there?

There are two main kinds of stocks; Common stock and preferred stock.

Common stock entitles owners to vote at shareholder meetings and receive dividends. While preferred stockholders usually don't have voting rights, but they receive dividend payments before common stockholders do, and have priority over common stockholders if the company goes bankrupt and its assets are liquidated.

Common and preferred stocks may fall into one or more of the following categories:

- Growth Stocks: Growth Stocks have earnings growing at a faster rate than the market average. They rarely pay dividends, and investors buy them in the hope of capital appreciation. A start-up technology company is likely to be a growth stock.
- Income Stocks: Income Stocks pay dividends consistently. Investors buy them for the income they generate. An established utility company is likely to be an income stock.
- Value stocks: These stocks have a low price-to-earnings (PE) ratio, meaning they are cheaper to buy than stocks with a higher PE. Value stocks may be growth or income stocks, and their low PE ratio may reflect the fact that they have fallen out of favor with investors for some reason. People buy value stocks in the hope that the market has over-reacted and that the stock's price will rebound.
- Blue-Chip Stocks: These are shares in large, well-known companies with a solid history of growth. They generally pay dividends.

Another way to categorize stocks is by the size of the company, as shown in its market capitalization. There are large-cap, mid-cap, and small-cap stocks. Shares in small companies are sometimes called "microcap" stocks. The very lowest priced stocks are known as "penny stocks." These companies may have little or no earnings. Penny stocks do not pay dividends and are highly speculative.

What are the benefits and risks of stocks?

Stocks offer investors the highest potential for growth (capital appreciation) over a long period. Investors willing to stick with stocks over long periods say fifteen (15) years, generally have been rewarded with strong, positive returns.

However, stock prices move down as well as up. There's no guarantee that the company whose stock you hold will grow and do well, so you can lose the money you invest in stocks. If a company goes bankrupt and its assets are liquidated, common stockholders are the last in line to share in the proceeds. The company's bondholders will be paid first, then holders of preferred stock. If you are a common stockholder, you get whatever is left, which may be nothing. Even when companies aren't in danger of failing, their stock price may fluctuate (up or down). For example, large-company stocks as a group lost money on average about one out of every three years. If you have to sell shares on a day when the stock price is below the price you paid for the shares, you will lose money on the sale. Market fluctuations can be unnerving to some investors. A stock's price can be affected by factors inside the company, such as a faulty product, or by events the company has no control over, such as political or market events.

How to buy and sell stocks

You can buy and sell stocks through:
- A direct stock plan
- A dividend reinvestment plan
- A discount or full-service broker
- A stock fund

Direct stock plans: Some companies allow you to buy or sell their stock directly through them without using a broker. This saves on commissions, but you may have to pay other fees to the plan, including if you transfer shares to a broker to sell them. Some companies limit direct stock plans to employees of the company or existing shareholders. Some require minimum amounts for purchases or account levels.

Direct stock plans usually will not allow you to buy or sell shares at a specific market price or at a specific time. Instead, the company will buy or sell shares for the plan at set times, such as daily, weekly, or monthly at an average market price. Depending on the plan, you may be able to automate your purchases and have the cost deducted automatically from your savings account.

Dividend reinvestment plans: These plans allow you to buy more shares of a stock you already own by reinvesting dividend payments into the company. You must sign an agreement with the company to have this done. (Check with the company or your brokerage firm to see if you will be charged for this service.)

Discount or full-service broker: Brokers buy and sell shares for customers for a fee, known as a commission.

Stock funds are another way to buy stocks. These are a type of mutual fund that invests primarily in stocks. Depending on its investment objective and policies, a stock fund may concentrate on a particular type of stock, such as blue chips, large-cap value stocks, or mid-cap growth stocks. Stock funds are offered by investment companies and can be purchased directly from them or through a broker or adviser.

Understanding Fees

Buying and selling stocks entail fees. A direct stock plan or a dividend reinvestment plan may charge you a fee for that service. Brokers who buy and sell stocks for you charge a commission. A discount brokerage charges lower commissions than what you would pay at a full-service brokerage. However, generally, you have to research and choose investments by yourself. A full-service brokerage costs more, but the higher commissions pay for investment advice based on that firm's research.

Avoiding Fraud

Stocks in public companies are registered with the SEC (Security Exchange Commission), and in most cases, public companies are required to file reports to the SEC quarterly and annually. Annual reports include financial statements that have been audited by an independent audit firm. Information on public companies can be found on the SEC's EDGAR system.

Shares

Shares represent a fraction of ownership in a business. A business may declare different types (or classes) of shares, each having distinctive ownership rules, privileges, or share values. The issuance of a stock certificate may document ownership of shares. A stock certificate is a legal document that specifies the number of shares owned by the shareholder and other specifics of the shares, such as; the par value if any of the class of the shares.

A person who owns a percentage of the share has the ownership of the firm in proportion to his share. The shares form stock. The stock of a firm is divided into shares, the total of which are stated at the time of business formation. Furthermore, additional shares may subsequently be authorized by existing shareholders and issued by the company. In some jurisdictions, each share of stock has a specific declared par value, which is a nominal accounting value used to represent the equity on the balance sheet of the corporation. However, in other jurisdictions, shares of stock may be issued without associated par value. In the United Kingdom, Republic of Ireland, South Africa, and Australia, stock can also refer to completely different financial instruments such as government bonds and all kinds of marketable securities.

Shareholder Rights

Although ownership of 50% of shares does result in 50% ownership of a company, it does not give the shareholder the right to use a company's building, equipment, materials, or other property. This is because the company is considered a legal person; thus, it owns all its assets itself. This is important in areas such as insurance, which must be in the name of the company and not the main shareholder. In most countries, boards of directors and company managers have a fiduciary responsibility to run the company in the interests of its stockholders.

Nonetheless, as Martin Whitman writes: "...it can safely be

stated that there does not exist any publicly traded company where management works exclusively in the best interests of OPMI (Outside Passive Minority Investor) stockholders. Instead, there are both "communities of interest" and "conflicts of interest" between stockholders (principal) and management (agent). This conflict is referred to as the principal-agent problem. It would be naive to think that any management would forego management compensation, and management entrenchment, just because some of these management privileges might be perceived as giving rise to a conflict of interest with OPMIs.

Even though the board of directors runs the company, the shareholder has some impact on the company's policy, as the shareholders elect the board of directors. Each shareholder typically has a percentage of votes equal to the percentage of shares he or she owns. So long as the shareholders agree that the management (agent) is performing poorly, they can select a new board of directors, which can then hire a new management team. However, in practice, genuinely contested board elections are rare. Board candidates are usually nominated by insiders or by the board of the directors themselves, and a considerable amount of stock is held or voted by insiders.

Owning shares does not mean responsibility for liabilities. If a company goes broke and has to default on loans, the shareholders are not liable in any way. However, all money obtained by converting assets into cash will be used to repay loans and other debts first, so that shareholders cannot receive any money unless and until creditors have been paid (often the shareholders end up with nothing).

Stock Exchange

A stock exchange is a bourse where stock brokers and traders can buy and sell shares of stock, bonds, and other securities. Many large companies have their stocks listed on a stock exchange. This makes the stock more liquid and more attractive to many investors. The exchange may also act as a guarantor of settlement. Other stocks may be traded "over the counter" (OTC), that is, through a dealer. Some large companies have their stock listed on more than one exchange in different countries to attract international investors. Stock exchanges may also cover other types of securities, such as fixed-interest securities bonds or less frequently derivatives, which are more likely to be traded over the counter.

HISTORY OF THE STOCK MARKET

There are varying versions of how the stock market began; this is one of them. In France, during the 12th century, the "courtiers de change" were concerned with managing and regulating the debts of agricultural communities on behalf of the banks. Nevertheless, because these men also traded with debts, they could be called the first brokers. A common misbelieve is that in the late 13th century Bruges, commodity traders gathered inside the house of a man called Van der Beurze, and in 1409 they became the "Brugse Beurse," institutionalizing what had been, until then an informal meeting. The family Van der Beurze had a building in Antwerp where those gatherings occurred. The Van der Beurze had Antwerp, like most of the merchants of that period, as their primary place for trading. The idea quickly spread around Flanders and neighboring countries, and "Beurzen" soon opened in Ghent and Rotterdam.

In the middle of the 13th century, Venetian bankers began to trade in government securities. In 1351 the Venetian government outlawed spreading rumors intended to lower the price of government funds. Bankers in Pisa, Verona, Genoa, and Florence also began trading in government securities during the 14th century. This was only possible because these were independent city-states not ruled by a Duke but a council of influential citizens. Italian companies were also the first to issue shares. Companies in England and the Low Countries followed in the 16th century. Around this time, a joint-stock company, one whose stock is owned jointly by the shareholders, emerged and became important for colonization of what Europeans called the "New World."

Birth of formal Stock Markets

In the 17th and 18th centuries, the Dutch pioneered several financial innovations that helped lay the foundation of the modern financial system. While the Italian city-states produced the first transferable government bonds. They did not develop the other ingredients necessary to produce a fully-fledged capital market, the stock market. In the early 1600s, the Dutch East India Company (VOC) became the first company in history to issue bonds and shares of stock to the general public. As Edward Stringham (2015) notes, "companies with transferable shares date back to classical Rome, but these were usually not enduring endeavors, and no considerable secondary market existed (Neal, 1997, p. 61)." Founded in 1602, the Dutch East India Company was

14

also the first joint-stock company to get a fixed capital stock. As a result of this, continuous trade in company stock occurred on the Amsterdam Exchange. After that, a lively trade in various derivatives, among which options and repos, emerged on the Amsterdam market. Dutch traders also pioneered 'short-selling' a practice that was banned by the Dutch authorities as early as 1610. Amsterdam based businessman Joseph de la Vega's "Confusion de Confusiones" (1688) was the earliest known book about stock trading and the first book on the inner workings of the stock market (including the stock exchange).

There are now stock markets in virtually every developed and most developing economies, with the world's largest markets in the United States, United Kingdom, Japan, India, China, Canada, Germany (Frankfurt Stock Exchange), France, South Korea, and the Netherlands. A good number of the differences between the exchanges on developed and developing country exchanges emanated from the colonial origins of the latter.

FINANCE

Finance is a field that is concerned with the allocation (investment) of assets and liabilities over space and time, often under conditions of risk or uncertainty. Finance can also be defined as the art of money management. Participants in the market aim to price assets based on their risk level, fundamental value, and their expected rate of return. Finance can be split into three sub-categories: public finance, corporate finance, and personal finance.

Areas of Finance

Personal finance: Personal finance may involve paying for education, financing durable goods such as real estate and cars, buying insurance, e.g., health and property insurance, investing, and saving for retirement. Personal finance may also involve paying for a loan or debt obligations. The six key areas of personal financial planning, as suggested by the Financial Planning Standards Board, are Financial position, adequate protection, tax planning, investment and accumulation goals, retirement planning, and estate planning.

Corporate Finance

Corporate finance deals with the sources of funding and the capital structure of corporations. It involves the actions that managers take to increase the value of the firm to the shareholders, and the tools and analysis used to allocate financial resources. Although it is in principle different from managerial finance, which studies the financial management of all firms, rather than corporations alone. The main concepts in the study of corporate finance apply to the financial problems of all kinds of firms. Corporate finance generally involves balancing risk and profitability, while attempting to maximize an entity's assets, net income cash flow, and the value of its stock. It generically entails three primary areas of capital resource allocation. In the first, "capital budgeting," management must choose which "projects" (if any) to undertake. The discipline of capital budgeting may employ standard business valuation techniques or even extend to real options valuation. The second, "sources of capital," relates to how these investments are to be funded. Investment capital can be provided through different sources, some of which include; Shareholders, in the form of equity (privately or via an initial public offering), creditors, often in the form of bonds, and the firm's operations (cash flow). Short term funding or working capital is mostly provided by banks extending a line of credit. The balance between these elements forms the company's capital structure. The third, "the dividend policy," requires management to determine whether any unappropriated profit or excess cash is to be retained for future investment or distributed to shareholders, and if so, in what form. Short term financial management is often termed "working capital management" and relates to cash, inventory, and debtors management. Corporate finance also includes within its scope of business valuation, stock investing, or investment management.

Public Finance

Public finance describes finance as related to sovereign states and sub-national entities (states/provinces, counties, municipalities, etc.) and related public entities (e.g., school districts) or agencies. It usually encompasses a long-term strategic perspective regarding investment decisions that affect public entities. These long-term strategic periods usually encompass five or more years. Public finance is primarily concerned with:

- Identification of the required expenditure of a public sector entity

- Source(s) of that entity's revenue
- The budgeting process
- Debt issuance (municipal bonds) for public works projects

Central banks, such as the Federal Reserve System banks in the United States and Bank of England in the United Kingdom, are strong players in public finance, acting as lenders of last resort as well as strong influencers on monetary and credit conditions in the economy. Capital, in the financial sense, is the money that gives the business the power to buy goods to be used in the production of other goods or the offering of a service. Capital has two types of sources, equity and debt. The budget decides the deployment of capital. This may include the objective of the business, targets set, and results in financial terms, e.g., the target set for sale, resulting cost, growth, and required investment to achieve the planned sales, and financing source for the investment. A budget may be long term or short term. Long term budgets have a time horizon of five to ten years giving a vision to the company while short term is an annual budget that is drawn to control and operate in that particular year. Budgets will include proposed fixed asset requirements and how these expenditures will be financed. Capital budgets are often adjusted annually and should be part of a longer-term Capital Improvements Plan.

A cash budget is also required. The working capital requirements of a business are monitored at all times to ensure that there are sufficient funds available to meet short term expenses. The cash budget is a detailed plan that shows all expected sources and uses of cash when it comes to spending it appropriately. The cash budget has the following main sections:

- Beginning cash balance: Contains the last period's closing cash balance, in other words, the remaining cash of the previous year.
- Cash collections: This includes all expected cash receipts (all sources of cash for the period considered, mainly sales).
- Cash disbursements: Lists all planned cash outflows for the period, such as dividends, excluding interest payments on short-term loans, which appear in the financing section. All expenses that do not affect cash flow are excluded from this list, e.g., depreciation, amortization, etc.
- Cash excess or deficiency: A function of the cash needs and cash available. Cash needs are determined by the total cash disbursements plus the minimum cash balance required by company policy. If the total cash available is less than cash needs, a deficiency exists.
- Financing: Discloses the planned borrowings and repayments of those planned borrowings, including interest.

INVESTMENT

An investment is an acquisition of an asset with the hope that it will maintain or increase its value over time and give back a higher rate of return when it comes to disbursing dividends. In investment management, in choosing a portfolio, one has to use financial analysis to determine what, how much, and when to invest. To do this, a company must identify relevant objectives and constraints, which may include; institution or individual goals, time horizon, risk aversion, and tax considerations. When you invest, you are committing money or another resource in the expectation of some future benefit. For example; a college education can be considered an investment because you invest your time (a resource) in the hope of earning a degree and a good job after graduating (the future benefit). In finance, investing means that an individual commits money to a financial asset or security. This commitment could be either a stock or bond in the hope of receiving even more money later. The potential of receiving more money later is the reason why people invest in the first place.

How do Investments earn money?

Most investments bring in money through appreciation, interest payments, or dividends. Appreciation means that the value of an asset has increased. For example; if you purchased a collectible item for $100 and five years later, it was worth $500, then the collectible appreciated. Securities can do the same as a stock issued by a company that can increase in value over several years. A more suitable example is interest payments on loans. These interest payments you paid the lender were how the lender earned money on that loan or investment. One type of security that issues interest payments to its investors is a bond. When you buy a bond, you are lending money to the government or a corporation, who promises to pay you back and make interest payments on the amount you lent. Dividends are also issued as a payment to investors, but they are made by companies whose stock or equity you own. Public companies issue stock to raise money for business activities; this is done by letting investors purchase these stocks. If you own stock in a company, that company may also issue dividend payments to you as a way to share its profits with its investors. This is on top of any appreciation in the value of the stock.

Risks with Investing

Investing can earn money for you; however, it is not without risks. The most significant risk with investing is that you may lose the money you invested. Unlike savings or checking accounts, whose value is guaranteed by the Federal Deposit Insurance Corporation (FDIC), investments have no such guarantee. Particular investments are less risky than others, but all investments carry some amount of risk. The amount of risk also affects the rate of return of an investment, meaning for someone to take on a lot of risks, there must also be the possibility of great reward. One way that investors reduce their overall risk is by investing in a variety of different securities, such as stocks and bonds, or even in different types of the same security, such as government bonds and corporate bonds. This is known as diversification, and it's an essential concept for any investor to understand. Another significant risk in investing in your own emotions. Many investments are volatile in the short term, meaning that their value may fluctuate a lot over one to five years. During economic recessions, the value of many investments may fall drastically. As an investor, it is difficult to watch your investments lose money. This can lead to investment decisions based on fear or panic. Examples of such decisions may include selling stocks when the prices fall too low for your comfort. Keep this in mind that when you make investment decisions, you will perform better as an investor if your investment decisions are based on logic and reason rather than emotions.

Types of Investments

They include;

- Stocks
- Bonds/ Certificates of Deposit (CDs)
- Cryptocurrencies
- Real Estate
- Options
- Commodities

1. Stock: Companies sell stocks and in return, obtain cash. Selling stock means selling ownership of the company to an extent. However, this depends on the rights that are conferred to the investors purchasing stocks. Stocks are reclassified as common stock and preferred stock. Investors should diversify their portfolio by investing in various stocks based on their risk appetite, and if they are not able to make a proper investment decision, they should approach financial advisors.
2. Bonds: Bonds are fixed income instruments issued by a company in return for cash. An issuer of

bonds owes the holders of bonds a debt. The issuer has to pay interest or repay the principal amount at a later agreed date (maturity).

3. Options: An option contract is an arrangement between two parties where one party agrees to buy or sell a particular asset at a later agreed date. That means this agreement gives the buyer of "option" a right to buy/sell.

4. Real Estate: Real Estate means property, land, buildings, etc. The major benefit of investing in real estate would be that there would be wealth generation by means of appreciation in the value of the real estate assets. The major types of real estate include the following:

Residential real estate: examples are; houses, condominiums, vacation homes, etc. Commercial real estate: examples are shopping malls, schools, buildings, offices, hotels, etc. Industrial real estate: examples are; factories, manufacturing units, buildings used for research, production, storage, etc.

1. Cryptocurrencies: Cryptocurrency is a digital currency that has strong cryptography to secure financial transactions. They are used to verify and regulate the transfer of funds, generation of currency units. Examples of Cryptocurrencies investments are; Bitcoin, Litecoin, Ripple, Ethereum, Bitcoin Cash, Ethereum Classic, etc.

2. Commodities: Commodities investment examples include; precious metal bullion like gold, silver, platinum: Energy resources like crude oil, gas, or

natural resources like agricultural wood and timber products, etc.

There are different types of investments available in the market, like the ones stated above. Choosing the right type of investment is very important depending on the quantum of investment, the expectation from the investment, and the risk appetite of the investor. Investors are advised to seek professional help, avoid investments that are outside their understanding, and also try to diversify their portfolio to reduce the level of risk to its minimum.

PROS AND CONS OF STOCK MARKET INVESTING

Historically, the stock market has delivered generous returns to investors over time, but the stock market also goes down, presenting investors with the possibility for both profits and loss. Below are some of the merits and demerits of owning stocks.

Pros

1. Stock ownership takes advantage of a growing economy: As the economy grows, so do corporate earnings. That's because economic growth creates jobs, which creates income, which creates sales. The fatter the paycheck, the greater the boost to consumer demand, which drives more revenues into companies' cash registers. They are the best way to stay ahead of inflation. Historically, stocks have averaged an annualized return of 10 percent. That's better than the average annualized inflation rate of 3.2 percent. It does mean that you must have a longer time horizon. That way, you can buy and hold even if the value temporarily drops.

2. Easy to buy: The stock market makes it easy to buy shares from companies. You can purchase them through a broker, a financial planner, or online. Once you've set up an account, you can buy stocks

in minutes. Several online brokers, such as Robinhood, even let you buy and sell stocks today for free. You can make money in two ways. Most investors intend to buy low and then sell high. They invest in fast-growing companies that appreciate in value. That's attractive to both day traders and buy-and-hold investors. The first group hopes to take advantage of short term trends, while the latter expects to see the company earnings and stock price grow over time. They both believe their stock-picking skills allow them to outperform the market. Other investors prefer a regular stream of cash. They purchase stocks of companies that pay dividends. Those companies grow at a moderate rate.

3. They are easy to sell: The stock market allows you to sell your stock at any time. Economists use the term "liquid" to describe the fact that you can turn your shares into cash quickly and with low transaction costs. That's important if you suddenly need your money. Since prices are volatile, you run the risk of being forced to take a loss.

Cons

1. You could lose your entire investment: If a company does poorly, investors will sell, sending the stock price plummeting. When you sell, you will lose your initial investment. If you can't afford to lose your initial investment, then you should buy bonds. You get an income tax break if you lose money on your stock loss. Unfortunately, you also

have to pay taxes if you make money. You pay the capital gains tax.

2. Stockholders are paid last if the company goes broke: Preferred stockholders and bondholders/creditors get paid first. Nevertheless, this happens only if a company goes bankrupt. A well-diversified portfolio should keep you safe if anyone company goes under.

3. It requires a lot of time: You have to research every company to determine how profitable you think it will be before you buy stock. You also have to learn how to read financial statements, annual reports, and follow your company's developments in the news. You also have to monitor the stock market itself, as even the best company's price will fall in a market correction or market crash.

4. It can be an emotional roller coaster: Stock prices rise and fall every second. Individuals tend to buy high, out of greed, and sell low, out of fear. The best thing to do is don't always look at the price fluctuations of stocks; just be sure to check in regularly.

5. You compete against professionals: Institutional investors and professional traders have more time and knowledge to invest. They also have sophisticated trading tools, financial models, and computer systems at their disposal.

As an individual investor, you must find out how to always be at an advantage. A well-diversified portfolio will provide most of the benefits and fewer disadvantages than stock ownership alone. This means you should have a mix of stocks, bonds, and commodities.

SUCCESS STORIES AND TIPS TO BECOME A SUCCESSFUL INVESTOR

The best investors in the world use simple common-sense approaches that have been making them money for years. Each has a simple systematic approach that they've stuck too over the years (except Peter Lynch; Lynch changes his style with the times). Their philosophies and investment styles may surprise new investors.

Below are some of the names of the world most successful stock market investors:

1. Warren Buffett: The name Warren Buffett is one of the well-known names in finance. His name always appears on the top of lists touting the world's wealthiest and most philanthropic, solidifying his place as one of the top investors in the world. To his investment colleagues, he is known as the "Oracle" or "Sage of Omaha" and has long been thought of as one of the most successful investors in history. Despite his $39 billion fortune, he is known for his frugal lifestyle, which transcends into his business practices. His philosophy is simple and stems around two rules: Don't lose money and Don't forget rule number one.

Buffet maintains his role at the helm of Berkshire Hathaway, the holdings company, which he turned from a floundering textile company into the successful conglomerate it is today. He has pledged to donate 99% of his fortune to charity either during his life or upon his death.

1. John Templeton: Taking the premise of buy low and sell high to the extreme, John Templeton, one of the most famous investors, took risks on companies' others would have shied away from. In 1939, John borrowed money and boldly invested in 100 companies, most of which were on the brink of bankruptcy. However, He exercised some caution by never spending more than one hundred dollars per share. His bold moves paid off, and he ended up selling all but four of the companies for a substantial profit. He followed this investment strategy throughout his career, often picking stocks that were widely ignored by other brokers and turning small investments into millions of dollars. This Strategy helped Templeton become a hugely successful investor. He was a savvy networker, using his contacts on Wall Street to gain valuable investment data, which he later would use to analyze his portfolio. In the 60s, Templeton moved to the Bahamas, where he became a naturalized British citizen, and in light of his financial and philanthropic endeavors, queen Elizabeth II knighted him. He died in 2008, but Sir John Templeton's legacy lives on through his philanthropy and his foundation, which awards millions of dollars each year in scholarships and grants.

2. Philip Fisher: Philip Fisher was known throughout the industry as the Father of Growth Investments because he often took the buy and hold approach. In 1955 he strategically purchased shares of Motorola stock, which he saw to be a high

potential growth company. Fisher still owned shares when he died in 2004. He theorized that to be a successful investor, it was best not over to diversify but rather know a few companies and know them well. Fisher was a witty networker, using his contacts to gain as much information about a company as possible. This he did to validate his investment moves. Fisher penned several books on his investment strategies, including his first investment book, 'Common Stocks and Uncommon Profits,' which is one of the first to ever to make the New York Times Best Sellers List. His works are still studied today by investment professionals.

3. Benjamin Graham: He is recognized by his peers and those within the investment industry as the father of security analysis and value investing. Graham's 'common-sense' approach was much more than mere common sense. His primary philosophy stemmed around the principle that investments should only be made if they are worth substantially more than they cost. Coining the phrase "margin of safety," Graham sought out companies that had little debt, above-average profit margins, and substantial cash flow. He was cognizant of the market's volatility and was able to use that knowledge to earn a profit. He knew that fluctuations in the market are inevitable and can be advantageous by buying when there is a bargain to be held (i.e., a reliable company, performed weakly in the market) and selling when the holdings are overvalued. Graham often used the analogy Mr.

Market, an imaginary partner to every investor, to illustrate the movement in the market. Graham died in 1976 but is still heralded by many as a leader in modern investing. He authored two of the most famous investment books of all time, 'Security Analysis' and 'The Intelligent Investor.'

4. Peter Lynch: When it comes to successful business investors, Peter Lynch is second to none. Over 13 years, Lynch managed the Fidelity Magellan fund, whose assets grew from $20 million to $14 billion. Like a chameleon, his investment strategy adapts to suit the nature of the asset. Lynch, the quintessential workaholic, had a philosophy that, if followed, could enable new investors out-perform Wall Street. After extensive and thorough research, Lynch would only invest in stocks he understood. As an investor, he was knowledgeable about the market and its volatility. He avoided long shots, was quick to learn from his own mistakes, and he was always able to explain the reasons behind a purchase. Lynch is heralded as one of the biggest success stories on Wall Street. He is currently serving as the vice-chairman of Fidelity Management & Research Company and is working with a variety of philanthropic endeavors. One of Lynch's favorite quotes states; "Don't be afraid to change things up, but always be able to explain why Knowledge is power."

5. George Soros: George Soros is a heavy investing weight, rising to fame in the early '90s on the back of his bet against the Bank of England. The hedge fund maverick made one billion dollars in a single

month by betting against the British pound at a time when the Bank of England artificially propped up the currency. Soros is an old school and embraces the unpredictable nature of investing in markets. A gambler at heart, he specializes in taking highly leveraged bets or making investments using borrowed cash to capitalize on macroeconomic trends. He's a big believer in doing the research, then following his gut instinct.

6. Jack Bogle: Bogle is the man who pioneered low-cost index investing for millions of people by founding the Vanguard Group in 1974, which created the first index fund, the Vanguard 500. Bogle was one of the first to forgo the individual stock picking strategy in favor of a broadly diversified portfolio made up of index funds, held over a long period. Bogle's legacy and contribution to finance and cements his reputation as one of the world's top investors.

7. Carl Icahn: Carl Icahn is likely the most significant activist investor and one of the most famous investors of our time. He likes to get his hands dirty and is a specialist in buying up companies he thinks are poorly managed, before turning them around for a quick profit. His strategy involves getting on the board of companies he invests in; then, he cleans the house. He'll either get the company making money again or break it up and sell off the profitable parts. He's such a successful business investor that mere rumors of his involvement are enough to get other investment managers buying up shares of said company,

raising the stock price. This phenomenon is known as the Icahn Lift.

8. Bill Ackman: Bill Ackman is often compared with Carl Icahn because they are both activist investors. Out of the top business investors, Ackman isn't afraid to voice his opinions. He correctly predicted the 2008 recession and is famous for his high profile bet against Herbalife going so far as to call them out for operating a pyramid scheme. Ackman has an incredible track record, turning $50 million into $12 billion with Pershing Square Capital. That sort of return places him firmly in the pantheon of the most successful investors of all time.

9. Peter Thiel: Peter Theil is an alien. Successful investors come in all shapes and forms. Thiel is a bit different from the others because rather than investing in the market, he became an entrepreneur and angel investor. The man co-founded not one, but two multibillion-dollar companies (PayPal and Palantir), and he was the first person to invest in Facebook. Thiel touches on his investment philosophy in his book Zero to One, where he talks about how a successful business should have some monopoly. He brings up Google as an example, a company that has a monopoly in search.

10. Ray Dalio: Dalio, one of the walls streets best investors, is the world's most successful hedge-fund managers. He's the world's 88th richest human and boasts an estimated personal fortune of $15 billion. His company, Bridgewater Associates, is the world's largest hedge fund and has around $160 billion in assets. He's been called Wall

Street's Oddest Duck for his unique management style. He runs his company as a strict meritocracy where employees are encouraged to be up-front at all times and tear down other's ideas in search of the "truth." The company has done exceptionally well, throwing up an annualized return of 14% since 1991. Dalio's strategy is to take numerous uncorrelated bets in markets all over the world. An uncorrelated bet means that a bet going south in one market isn't affected by or does not affect a bet in another market. It's essentially another way of saying that they diversify their portfolio super well. Dalio splits the market into two: growth and inflation; each segment is then divided into two again, depending on whether the variable in question is rising or falling. He then tries to make sure he is equally distributed in all four categories. This strategy has helped Dalio become one of the top investors in the world.

11. Prince Alwaleed: The Saudi Arabian prince, is one of the most influential business investors. He is worth more than $20 billion and has investments across a wide range of interests. Some of which include; banking, entertainment, retail, petrochemicals, and transportation. He is the founder and CEO of Kingdom Holding Company, an investment company based in Saudi Arabia. Often referred to as the Saudi Warren Buffett, he favors high-growth, high-risk tech companies and has ownership over an extensive collection of luxury hotels such as the Savoy in London and Plaza in New York. Legend has it that the Prince

turned a $15,000 inheritance in 1979 (worth about $50,000 today) and a house that he mortgaged for $400,000 into a $20 billion+ empire. The recession was a difficult time, as his company lost 65% of its capital and had to move some of his own money into the investment company. His stake in Citibank suffered the most, falling in value by $6 billion. He's made a comeback since then, and Kingdom Holding Company is one of the largest foreign investors in the U.S.

Above are philosophical strategies of the trade from some of the world's most famous investors. However, it's up to you to use what method works best for your money and always be smart and diligent when it comes to investing.

THE MOST IMPORTANT THING: YOUR MINDSET

INVESTOR'S MINDSET

According to Warren Buffet, "A successful investor invests in great things, focuses on its earnings but makes volatility his/her friend." Many at times, when we invest in a stock, the biggest urge is to sell as soon as possible and book profit. In some cases, people have this temptation to sell early because of the speculation that the market might fall, and the value of their investments will also fall. In other cases, people have this dilemma that if they don't ever sell an investment, they will not be able to make money and that money is only made by selling the investments. The utility of an asset doesn't change drastically because the volatility in the price of that asset is very limited. However, sometimes, because of crowd behavior, even the prices of great things become highly bloated, and a successful investor should take advantage of such situations. Earnings of an asset usually stay stable most of the time, but sometimes change in the sentiment can cause significant disruptions in price. As an investor, you should keep an eye on the utility of an asset and try to gauge the optimum value for the utility. Your focus as an investor should be on buying great companies with calculated projections that the earnings of those companies will grow in the future.

Sometimes, the price of these great companies might grow drastically above their earning abilities and vice versa giving a chance to investors to either sell or invest in these companies to take advantage of the market euphoria. When you buy, you cannot time the market with regards to price and anticipate a boom or a bust, but if you buy great businesses, then even if no boom or burst occurs during the lifetime of the investment, those investments will still grow because of increased earnings.

As an investor, you are to think like an owner. The focus of the owner is not on the price but on how to increase the earnings on year by year basis. This is because if earnings grow for a more extended period, the price will surely follow. In Warren Buffet's words, "In the short run, stock markets behave like voting machines, but in the long run, they behave like weighing machines." This means that in the short run, the price of a stock might fluctuate because of P/E or other factors, but in the long run, it is driven by the earnings of the company. Furthermore, Benjamin Graham quotes that the first thing which a typical investor should think when he/she buys a stock is to believe that he/she has bought part of a business.

Below are four different money mindsets of investing

1. People who prefer to give their investment capital to someone else: These set of people are intentionally unconscious about investing because they believe that they are busy with other things that are more interesting to them. As such, they give their money to a mutual fund manager and

take mutual fund investment advice from someone who gives an agreed percentage return on the money invested. He or She probably won't get the return he deserves by having someone else manage his money and also doesn't know what companies his money is invested in.

2. People who don't want to learn to invest: These set of people don't believe they can do it. They are intentionally unconscious about investing because they think it's hard to learn or not worth the effort. The beautiful thing about compound interest is that it keeps working when you aren't. You have to put forth a little effort up front, but in the long run, you get to watch your money grow in the stock market.

3. People who have no money or think they don't have enough money: These people think they need money to be an investor and are unintentionally unconscious about investing money. They are unaware of the fact that they can learn to invest without a ton of money.

4. People who are learning or have learned to invest: These people have learned to be conscious and awake about their money. They have successfully debunked the most common myths of investing that states;

· Only experts can invest

· You can't beat the market

· You need to diversify

These set of people have come to understand that they need to invest to be financially independent and also have a blissful retirement. It is also important to note that people that have stock market success have a positive relationship with money. They are not obsessed with money, but respectful and appreciative. They want it for what it can do for them as a part of their investor life. They want to put money to work for their benefit. The best stock market investors see the market and investing as a great social game. Like all investing, stock markets are parts of the social game of life. Markets are places that exchange, influence, and sometimes even control perceptions. Markets are perception. Accepting and understanding these puts you well on the way to stock market success. Stock market success yields return in money. Money builds financial freedom, which provides options. It gives you more control over time. Well managed money contributes to peace of mind and comfort.

Furthermore, the successful investor mind begins by knowing yourself. It is also essential to know your stock market. This awareness builds your investor's mind and sets you on the way to an investor's life. To know your stock market, review your thinking and investing attitudes. Know, understand, and regulate them. Improving knowledge helps improve investing results. That applies to both do it yourself, investors, and clients of financial advisors. It takes time to learn, but you can learn at your own pace. Also, as you learn, you can take more control of your investments and financial future.

RULES THAT WARREN BUFFET LIVES BY

Berkshire Hathaway CEO Warren Buffett is arguably the world's greatest stock investor. He is also a bit of a philosopher. Buffett pares down his investment ideas into simple, memorable sound bites. Warren Buffett is the third richest person in the world, with a net worth of over $85 billion. He is regarded by some as the best stock picker in the world, with his investment philosophies and guidelines influencing numerous investors. One of his most famous sayings is "Rule No. 1: Never lose money. Rule No. 2: Never forget rule No. 1." Another one is; "If the business does well, the stock eventually follows." The third is, "It's far better to buy a wonderful company at a fair price than a fair company at a wonderful price." Buffett personally lost about $23 billion in the financial crisis of 2008, and his company, Berkshire Hathaway, lost its revered AAA ratings. How can he then say; 'never lose money.' By saying an investor should never lose money, he is referring to the mindset of a sensible investor. He is also saying; don't be frivolous and don't gamble. Don't go into an investment with a cavalier attitude that it's okay to lose. Be informed and, more importantly, do your homework. Buffett invests only in companies he thoroughly researches and understands. He doesn't go into an investment prepared to lose, and neither should you. Buffett believes the essential quality for an investor is temperament, not intellect. A successful investor doesn't focus on being with or against the crowd. The stock market will experience swings. However, in good and bad times, Buffett stays focused on his goals, and so should you. This esteemed investor rarely changes his long-term investing strategy no matter what the market does. "If the business does well, the stock eventually follows."

"The Intelligent Investor" by Benjamin Graham convinced Buffett that investing in a stock equates to owning a piece of the business. So, when he searches for a stock to invest in, Buffett seeks out businesses that exhibit favorable long-term prospects. He does this by asking salient questions such as; does the company have a consistent operating history? Does it have a dominant business franchise? Is the business generating high and sustainable profit margins? If the company's share price is trading below expectations for its future growth, then it's a stock Buffett may want to own.

Buffett never buys anything unless he can write down the reasons why he'll pay a specific price per share for a particular company. Do you do the same? They don't call him "The Oracle" for nothing. "It's far better to buy a wonderful company at a fair price than a fair company at a wonderful price." Buffett is a value investor who likes to buy quality stocks at rock bottom prices. His real goal is to build more and more operating power for Berkshire Hathaway by owning stocks that will generate reliable profits and capital appreciation for years to come. When the markets reeled during the 2007-2008 financial crisis, Buffett was stock piling great long-term investments by investing billions in names like General Electric and Goldman Sachs. To pick stocks well, investors must set down criteria for uncovering good businesses and stick to their discipline. You might, for example, seek companies that offer a durable product or service, and also have stable operating earnings and the germ for future profits. You might establish a minimum market capitalization you're willing to accept, and a maximum P/E ratio or debt level. Finding the right company at the right price with a margin for safety against unknown market risk is the ultimate goal. Remember, the price you pay for a stock isn't the same as the value you get. Successful investors know the difference.

Warren Buffett's net worth as of June 2019 is $85 billion, which makes him the third richest person in the world. "Our favorite holding period is forever." How long should you hold a stock? Buffett says if you don't feel comfortable owning a stock for 10 years, you shouldn't own it for 10 minutes. Even during the period, he called the "Financial Pearl Harbor," Buffett loyally held on to the bulk of his portfolio. Unless a company has suffered a sea change in prospects, such as impossible labor problems or product obsolescence, a long holding period will keep an investor from acting too human. Being too fearful or too greedy can cause investors to sell stocks at the bottom or buy at the peak and destroy portfolio appreciation for the long run.

Below are three rules that have helped Warren Buffett (the Oracle of Omaha) attain and sustain success:

1. Practice excellent communication: To become like Warren Buffet, you need to develop excellent communication skills if you want to lead. Buffett's first key to prosperity has little to do with picking stocks. He says you need to become a strong communicator. Wield words as your most important tools. Buffett once told a Stanford MBA

student, he said; "Without good communication skills, you won't be able to convince people to follow you even though you see over the mountain, and they don't." While this is sage advice for financial planners, it's good for helping anyone develop leadership skills and the ability to think in stressful situations.

2. Live frugally: For a billionaire, Buffett is known to live a surprisingly frugal life. Buffett famously lives well below his means. He has been known to drive an older, modest car. He still resides in the house he bought in Omaha, Nebraska, for $31,500 in 1958, and he picks up breakfast at a McDonald's almost every day. Think of wealth as security, not a license to spend foolishly. Live modestly, and you'll be able to weather dip in the financial markets. An automated investing service can help you stay calm too. If you invest in feeding a lavish lifestyle, you'll soon find yourself making rash decisions based on greed.

3. Always be willing to learn new things: knowledge is power. The amount of information you have determines the rate and pace at which you will make progress. As an investor who hopes to someday become successful like Buffet, you have to acquire as much knowledge as you can about the stock market and also the company before investing.

INVESTOR VERSUS TRADER

Trading is a method of holding stocks for a short time. It could be for a week or more often a day. Traders hold stocks for the short-term high performance. Investing, on the other hand, is an approach that works on buy and hold a principle. Investors invest their money for some years, decades, or even more extended periods. Short term market fluctuations are insignificant in the long-running investing approach. When it comes to wealth creation in the equity market, investing and trading is the two genres of the field. However, investing and trading is very different approaches to wealth creation or generating profits in the financial market. Imagine, today, you and your friend bought an equal amount of seeds to sow in your fields, but you sold them to someone in a day because you could earn a profit. Also, your friend sowed the seeds and let them grow for a few years till they gave new seeds. He sowed the new seeds and continued this for years and sold a lot more seeds eventually than were bought. By investing his seeds, he would have made profit quite different than what you made by trading your seeds. This is simply the difference in investing and trading.

Furthermore, traders look at the price movement of stocks in the market. If the price goes higher, traders may sell the stocks. Trading is a skill of timing the market, whereas investing is an art of creating wealth by compounding interest and dividend over the years by holding quality stocks in the market. Undoubtedly, both trading and investing imply risk in your capital. However, trading comparatively involves higher risk, and higher potential returns as the price might go high or low in a short while. Since investing is an art, it takes a while to develop. It involves comparatively lower risk and lower returns in the short run but might deliver higher returns by compounding interests and dividends if held for a longer period.

Daily market cycles do not affect much on quality stock investments for a longer time. Traders put money in stock for the short term. They buy and sell fast to hit higher profits in the market. Missing the right time may lead to a loss. They look at the present performance of the companies to hit the higher price and book profits in the short term. Whereas, investors keep themselves away from the trends and invest in value. They invest for a longer period keeping an eye on the stocks they hold. They patiently wait until the stock reaches its potential. Ultimately, the ones who achieve their financial goals are successful.

PLAN TOMORROW TODAY

"We have long felt that the only value of stock forecasters is to make fortune-tellers look good." (Warren Buffett)

What does this mean? It means no one can control how the market will act tomorrow. However, we can control how we react to the market. Understanding our natural tendency to value today over tomorrow is a big step towards managing our future better. When the market has another pull back, you will recall that you are investing in the future. Preparation raises our probability of success, not only in the monetary sense but also emotionally. Investing for tomorrow today, for instance; If you had the choice

45

between receiving $1,000 today or $1,050 tomorrow, which option would you choose? If your answer is $1,000 today, congratulations! You are normal. What if you had the choice between $1,000 a year from today or $1,050 366 days from now, which option would you choose then? If you went with $1,050 366 days from now, congratulations! You are normal. Why not wait an extra day since you already waited 365 days? What are the difference between the 24 hours, today, and tomorrow when compared to the 24 hours between 365 and 366 days from now? Eventually, that future day 365 will become today, so why do most people answer differently to each of these questions? The answer is what smart people call time preference and our myopic time inconsistency. Research indicates that humans tend to value today more than tomorrow, tomorrow's tomorrow, and the tomorrow after that. In fact, our value of each future date diminishes one calendar page at a time, with our retired selves getting the least amount of importance. We think of our future selves as different people, akin to a stranger sitting across the poker table. Could this today centric view of ourselves be the core driver behind 25% American workers having less than $1000 saved for retirement? Alternatively, why almost half of all baby boomers have less than $25,000? There are enough physical and mental hurdles to overcome when generally thinking long term, let alone implementing a specific financial plan.

EMOTIONS VERSUS FACTS AND STRATEGIES

Emotion is ever-present in the stock market. Feelings do not discriminate among amateur and professional investors.

Even though some people have more practice than others at keeping their emotions in check when making financial decisions. Nonetheless, positive and negative feelings do creep into the stock market and affect the stock market performance. These emotional extremes can trigger irrational decision making that may cost investors money. While in some cases, joy can actually work to a stock's advantage. There is an emotional pain that is associated with the financial loss that can cause investors to continue holding losing stocks out of fear. Emotional investing is not limited to the small investor. Indeed, investment professionals, such as traders, struggle with emotion, including fear when navigating the stock market. Professional traders are often aware of their weaknesses. As such, they have strategic measures in place to help them control their fear of financial loss.

Facts about the stock market

1. Buy low, sell high.
2. There is no such thing as a sure thing.
3. Get familiar with filings.
4. Think long term.
5. Dividends are your friends.
6. There is no perfect metric.
7. A $100 stock isn't expensive, and a $5 stock isn't cheap.
8. Taxes can take a bite out of your profits.
9. Know what you need and what you're paying for.
10. Take market "news" with a whole shaker of salt.

Stock investment strategies

There are several different ways to approach stock investing, but nearly all of them fall under one of three basic styles. They include; value investing, growth investing, or index investing. These stock investment strategies follow the mindset of an investor, and the strategy they utilize to invest is affected by several factors, such as the investor's financial situation, investing goals, and risk tolerance.

1. Value Investing Basics: The strategy of value investing, in simple terms, means buying stocks of companies that the market place has undervalued. The goal is not to invest in no-name companies that haven't been recognized for their potential that falls more in the venue of speculative or penny stock investing. Value investors typically buy into strong companies that are trading at low prices that an investor believes don't reflect the company's true value. Value investing is all about getting the best deal, similar to getting a great discount on a designer brand. When we say that a stock is undervalued, we mean that an analysis of their financial statements indicates that the price the stock is trading at is lower than it should be, based on the company's intrinsic value. This might be indicated by things such as a low price-to-book ratio (a financial ratio favored by value investors) and a high dividend yield, which represents the amount in dividends a company pays out each year relative to the price of each share. The market

place is not always correct in its valuations, and thus, stocks often trade for less than their true worth, at least for a period. If you pursue a value investing strategy, the goal is to seek out these undervalued stocks and scoop them up at a favorable price.

Value Investing Long Term: The value investing strategy is pretty straight forward, but practicing this method is more involved than you might think, especially when you're using it as a long-term strategy. It's essential to avoid the temptation to try to make fast cash based on flighty market trends. A value investing strategy is based on buying into strong companies that will maintain their success, and that will eventually have their intrinsic worth recognized by the markets. Warren Buffet, one of the greatest and most prolific value investors of the century, famously said, "In the short term, the market is a popularity contest. In the long term, a market is a weighing machine." Buffet bases his stock choices on the true potential and stability of a company. He looks at each company as a whole instead of merely looking at an undervalued price tag that the market has assigned individual shares of the company's stock. However, he does still prefer to buy stocks he perceives as "on-sale."

1. The Basics of Growth Stock Investment Strategies: For decades, growth investing has been held as the yin to value investing's yang. While growth investing is in the most basic terms, the so-called "opposite" of value investing, many value investors also employ a growth investing mindset when

settling on stocks. In the long term, growth investing is very similar to value stock investing strategies. Basically, if you're investing in stocks based on the intrinsic value of a company and its potential to grow in the future, you're using a growth investing strategy. Growth investors are distinguished from value investors by their focus on young companies that have shown their potential for significant, above-average growth. Growth investors look at companies that have repeatedly shown indications of growth and substantial or rapid increase in business and profit. The general theory behind growth investing is that an increase in share prices will then reflect the growth in earnings or revenue a company generates. Differing from value investors, growth investors may often buy stocks priced at or higher than a company's current intrinsic worth, based on the belief that a continued high growth rate will eventually boost the company's intrinsic value to a substantially higher level well above the current share price of the stock.

Popular financial metrics used by growth investors include; earnings per share (EPS), profit margin, and return on equity (ROE) (A Fusion of Value and Growth). As Buffet effectively employs, if you're considering a long-term approach to investing, a fusion of value and growth investing may be worth your consideration. There are good reasons to back up taking these stock investment strategies. Historically, value stocks are usually the stocks of companies in cyclical industries, which are primarily made up of businesses producing goods and services that people use their discretionary income on. The airline industry is a good example; people fly more when the business cycle is on an uptrend and fly less when it swings downward because they have more and less discretionary income, respectively.

As a result of this season, value stocks typically perform well in the market during times of economic recovery and prosperity. However, they are likely to fall behind when a bull market is sustained for an extended period of time. Growth stocks typically perform better when interest rates drop, and companies' earnings take off. They are also typically the stocks that continue to rise even in the late stages of a long-term bull market. On the other hand, these are usually the first stocks to take a beating when the economy slows down. A fusion of growth and value investing offer investors the opportunity to enjoy higher returns on investment while reducing a substantial amount of risk. Theoretically, if an investor employs both a value investing strategy for buying some stocks while using a growth investing strategy for buying other stocks, he/she can generate optimal earnings during virtually any economic cycle, and any fluctuations in returns will be more likely to balance out over time in his/her favor.

1. Passive Index Investing: Index investing is a much more passive form of investing when compared to that of either value or growth investing. Consequently, it involves far less work and strategizing on the part of the investor. Index investing diversifies an investor's money widely

among various types of equities. This is done with the hope to mirror the same returns as the overall stock market. One of the main attractions of index investing is that studies have shown that few strategies of picking individual stocks outperform index investing over the long term. An index investing strategy is usually followed by investing in mutual funds or exchange-traded funds that are designed to reflect the performance of a major stock index such as the S&P 500 or the FTSE 100.

Conclusively, investors have to discover their stock investment strategies that best suit their individual wants or needs, as well as their investment "personality." As an investor, you may discover that combining the three approaches, as discussed above, is what works best for you. Also, the investing strategy or strategies you employ will often change during your life as your financial situation, and goals change. Don't be afraid to shake things up a bit and diversify how you invest, but strive always to maintain a firm grasps on what your investment approach entails and how it will likely affect your portfolio and your finances.

BE MORE PRODUCTIVE NOT BUSIER

'Busy' means the focus is on how much time one is spending on something. While 'productive' means making the results the priority. Also, Busy could mean multi-tasking, while productive means focusing on one thing at a time.

Below are some pieces of investment advice from Warren Buffett

· Risk comes from not knowing what you're doing: People talk about how much risk the stock market entails. They say things like; It's just too easy to lose money. Of course, it's got risks involved. But so does depend on one employer who could go bankrupt or let you go at any time. So how do you manage risks in the stock market? Buffett suggests that to know what you're doing, you have to learn. The more you understand it, the better you will be at it. The fact is, someone's sitting in the shade today because someone planted a tree a long time ago. The best time to invest is several years ago. The second-best time is now. The sooner you get in, the better. Don't wait to buy stocks. Buy stocks and wait. Should you find yourself in a chronically leaking boat, energy devoted to changing vessels is likely to be more productive than energy devoted to patching leaks. In the aforementioned, Buffett is talking about the sink-cost fallacy. This is the idea that you've already put money into something, so you should keep striving to make money with the initial investment even if doing so is both risky and requires more time and money. If you got into a bad deal, it's better to count your loss and move on than to try to force your way into making something from nothing by dropping more resources into a lost cause.

· A public opinion poll is no substitute for thought: Rather than jump on the latest headline with the newest fad, it's better to think things through for yourself. Use your head and make wise choices based on your own analysis, not someone else's. Some stocks are never good options. It doesn't matter what the newspaper says. It doesn't matter what your friend has stock in the company. Some deals just aren't worth having, so avoid them. It's far better to buy an excellent company at a fair price than a fair company at a wonderful price. The wisdom here is that the focus should be more on the company itself than on the price of the stock. Not to say the price is irrelevant. But Buffett is emphasizing that a good price on a stock of a bad company is still a bad idea. What you want to look for in a good company and then buy it when the stock is priced well.

· I always knew I was going to be rich. I don't think I ever doubted it for a minute: These words are some of the wisest we can consider when it comes to investing. Buffett is dealing with mindset. You've got to know you are going to win. It may not be today. It may not happen the way you think it should. But deep down inside, you've got to know you will win. That will make all the difference.

SET YOUR GOALS

One of the keys to successful investing is to have a plan. Setting the right investment goals can go a long way to developing one that works for you.

Below are some tips that could help in setting the right investment goals

1. Know why you are investing: It always helps to know why you are doing something. Think about why you want to invest. Are you hoping to build up your nest egg? Do you want to quickly build up enough for a down payment on a home? Are you creating an income portfolio? Determine why you want to invest. Being able to point to a specific reason for investing can help you set the right goals

and can provide you with a way to stay motivated as you move forward.

2. Be Realistic: If you are creating an income portfolio with the help of dividend stocks, the chances are that you won't see significant income in 12 months. You need to be realistic with your investment goals. Whether you are investing money in a tax-advantaged retirement account elsewhere, you need to acknowledge the realities of your situation. The next few years could be volatile. However, over time, the market is likely to become better. In any case, you have to be realistic about your returns over time. The latest DALBAR survey points out that the S&P 500 returned 7.89 percent annually over the last 20 years. Expecting 10 percent returns might not be realistic. You also have to be realistic about what you can do right now. Don't grandly proclaim that you're going to invest $500 a month when you aren't even sure if you have enough money for groceries. Look at your situation and set goals that are realistic.

3. Break It Down: Break down your investment goals into achievable milestones. Investment success is hard to come by if you find yourself constantly frustrated about your lack of progress. Start out small, with a reasonable monthly goal of saving $100 a month to invest. Then, while you do this, look for ways to find more money in your budget by cutting spending or earning extra income. Make a plan to step up your investment to $150 a month after a couple of months, and then up to $200 a month beyond that. Also, keep your focus on

making slow, steady progress rather than amassing some specific amount years down the road. Instead of telling yourself you need $1 million in your retirement account, break it down to a monthly investment (with a realistic expectation of returns). This will make the goal much more manageable, and you'll set yourself up for success.

4. Start Simple, With Something, You Know: As you begin investing, start simple. Don't just jump into stock picking, or decide that you want to trade. Instead, begin with something simple that you know. Begin with a broad index fund. Make regular investments (use dollar-cost averaging to make the most of a smaller budget) to the index fund while you research other investments. As you find success with the simple stuff, and learn about more complex investments, you can slowly branch out. However, before you invest in any asset, you should understand how it works, and the forces that influence it. Staring simply allows you to find regular success with something you understand and make progress as you learn about other opportunities. Once you have established your foundation, you can branch out.

How to set your investment goals

Investing can be a very different experience for different types of investors.

Investors are very different from each other based on aspects such as; age, income, savings rate, and needs.

Setting your goal is a crucial part of becoming a successful investor. Goals are one of the most important aspects of investing. The markets are very complex. They offer all kinds of financial instruments that connect investors with companies. It allows investors to transfer their money to the future while gaining positive returns. Different investors have different needs, and therefore, their investment goals will be quite different. Setting your goals for investing requires some thorough thinking. An investor must think of himself today, and he also must think of himself in the future. His goal is to be the future self that he wishes to become, and he will have to choose the right strategy to help him achieve his goals. Setting a goal isn't a simple procedure. A good goal can be measured and achievable. The goal must be clear and understandable. For example, invest $5,000 in a health care ETF such as Health Care Select Sector SPDR ETF (XLV). A bad goal, for example, will be to achieve financial independence, as it is immeasurable. The goals should also be achievable. While it should be achievable, it shouldn't be too hard to achieve. It should be challenging yet do-able. It should also encourage you to devise a good strategy to achieve it. A good list of goals will contain a wide array of goals, which are challenging yet doable and measurable.

Furthermore, when you start setting your goals, you should first look at your personal information. The current personal information will have an impact on what you can achieve in the coming year and what you can achieve in the long term. Your age, marital status, and income are all crucial when you set your goals. Another important aspect when setting investment goals is the investment horizon.

When will you need your money? If you need it next year because you save for down payment on a house, you will have one kind of goal, strategy, and portfolio. If you need it in twenty (20) years for your retirement, you will set other goals and use a different strategy. The investment horizon is a crucial element. Some goals require time, not just time in the market, but your own free time. For example, looking for a better paying job, allocating time to a side hustle that will increase your income, or reading books about investing all require time. Therefore, you should know how much time you can spare when you set your goals.

It is important to set financial goals. At this point, you know how much time you must spare; you've taken into account your personal information and your investment horizon. Also, try sticking to goals you can control. For example, a total return goal has a lot to do with the markets, and not with you. On the other hand, allocating a certain amount of money into your brokerage account is a controllable goal. Use actual numbers when setting your goals. 'Maximizing my saving rate or saving as much as I can are very bad goals.' They can't be measured, and they are just too vague. Use numbers to turn vague goals into specific goals. Save 20% of my annual income and transfer $15,000 to my brokerage account are specific and measurable goals that can be followed throughout the year. When you set financial goals, take into account that failing is a possibility, set challenging goals but not too hard. Let's assume you want to invest $15,000 annually. At the end of the year, it's quite different if you saved $14,300, or you save $7,000. Each failure will give different insights, and understanding our failures is a crucial part of improving as investors. Don't be afraid of failing. Big corporations run by successful people also miss their goals; sometimes, it's the long-term vision that matters. Set goals can monitor them throughout the year. Goals should be continuously monitored, at least quarterly, and preferably monthly. If your goal is to invest a certain amount of money, you don't want to be surprised by the end of the year. Monitoring them allows you to put more effort into areas where you lag or prioritize your goals if you realize you can't reach them all.

In setting your goals, it is also essential to take into consideration non-financial goals. Money is only a means to an end for many. We aren't a corporation where the vague goal is to maximize profits. As human beings, we have more goals that fill our lives. From education to family and hobbies, a healthy list of goals should combine financial goals with non-financial goals. At the end of the day, our financial goal will support our non-financial goals. As an investor, ensure that your non-financial goals can live with the financial goals in harmony. If one of your financial goals is to save 50% of your income, and you also set a non-financial goal of traveling abroad twice, it will be very challenging unless your income is very high. Try to choose goals that will support each other. For example, education can support your investment skills and your financial goals in the process. Your non-financial goals should be measurable, as well. Do you want to lose weight? Set a weight goal. Do you want to read more? Set how many books you want to read throughout the year. The use of measurable goals will allow you to monitor your progress and will also let you see how well you did by the end of the year.

Goals require strategy. You have your list of goals, but how do you achieve them. There are several ways to achieve most goals. Each way is a strategy, and an investor should choose a strategy that best fits him. Ensure your strategy makes sense and works well for all your goals. For instance, don't choose a cost-cutting strategy to increase your saving rate if you know that your spouse will disagree or that at the moment, you can't trim costs significantly. At the end of the year, when you check if you reached your goals, try to understand if you failed goals because you were too ambitious or you tried the wrong strategy. If you were too ambitious, consider amending the goal, and if your strategy failed you, consider choosing a different strategy next year.

In conclusion, goals are crucial for investing. Every financial company sets them, and so should you. Understand your current position in life, think about what you want to achieve in the future, and make a list of financial and non-financial goals. Then choose strategies that will help you achieve these goals and start working on them.

GET MORE SLEEP (Eat Well, Sleep Well)

"Eat well, sleep well" is an adage that refers to the risk-return trade-off. It says that the type of security an investor chooses depends on whether he or she wants to generate high returns or have peace of mind. This trade-off can be thought of as balancing return needs and risk tolerance.

Buying high-risk securities offers the possibility of earning high returns ("eating well") while buying low-risk securities offers the possibility of earning reliable returns ("sleeping well").

Investors often must balance their return needs and goals with their individual risk tolerances. This tradeoff can be referred to as "eat well, sleep well." Spreading holdings across different asset classes and industries should theoretically enable investors to both eat and sleep well. When investors contemplate which securities to buy, they make their judgments based on what level of returns they require, as well as how much risk they want to take on. Risk-return is the relationship between the potential amount of return gained on an investment and the amount of risk an investor must accept to participate in that investment. The higher the return desired, the more risk the investor must accept. That is where the "eat well, sleep well" adage comes in. Investing in securities with high expected returns offers investors the potential to eat well, but also maybe lose out on sleep. This is due to their volatile nature and a higher probability of dishing out devastating losses. In contrast, investing in lower-risk assets helps to minimize the potential for loss and generate smoother returns. This enables investors to sleep better, at the expense of eating less. Each investor's risk tolerance is the most critical factor in constructing an investment portfolio. Investors often must balance their return needs and goals with their risk tolerances. This trade-off can be referred to as "eat well, sleep well."

Types of eating well, sleep well securities

Investments that generally guarantee the least stress are cash deposits, money market funds, certificates of deposits (CD), and Treasury-inflation protected securities (TIPS). Investors that buy these types of securities can sleep safely at night, knowing they are doubtful to lose the money they invested. On the flip side, they will also be aware that being so risk-averse means missing out on the much better potential returns offered by other securities. Those preferring to eat well, meanwhile, will move much further up the risk scale, investing in racier assets such as emerging markets and small-cap stocks. These kinds of investments are considered to be among the riskiest. As a result, the most capable of generating high returns and sleepless nights.

Eat well, sleep well method

A popular saying on Wall Street is that stocks let us eat well and bonds let us sleep well. This phrase is a little over-generalized. This is because there are some fixed-income investments out there, such as; junk bonds, that are riskier than investing in an index fund tracking stocks in the S&P 500. Nevertheless, it makes an important point about how investors can go about getting the best of both worlds. In theory, investors can build a portfolio made up of both eat well and sleep well securities. When done properly, allocating capital among different asset classes and industries helps to minimize risk and potentially increase gains. Diversification is important. Spreading holdings should insulate portfolios from the ups and downs of a single stock or class of securities.

Special Considerations

Every investor would love to double their capital overnight. However, few will be willing to take on the kind of risk involved. A lot also depends on age. The rule of thumb is that an investor should gradually reduce risk exposure over the years, switching to less volatile securities as he or she closes in on retirement. Risk tolerance may change over time, so it is important to revisit the topic periodically. In general, young people are advised to prioritize eating well, oversleeping well. Financial advisors argue that they have time on their side to ride out market volatility and should look to amass the biggest amount of funds for later in life. That emphasis gradually changes as the person gets older and needs more money to cater to his/her needs.

LONG TERM INVESTING

Warren Buffett has time and again emphasized on long term investment benefits. His quote, "If you aren't thinking about owning a stock for ten (10) years, don't even think about owning it for ten (10) minutes" foregrounds the gravity of importance on holding a stock for a long term. When we talk about long term equity investments, we refer to a time frame that is within the minimum of six/seven years. This kind of investment has historically proven to generate more wealth than short term investments. Several factors make long term investment returns stand out than short term investment returns.

Benefits of long-term investment

One of the critical factors associated with long term investment is lower volatility rate. Since stocks are (highly) volatile, investing for a more extended period enables you to sustain and manage low market periods. Also, in such a case, you do not have to frown over falling stock market prices. Holding stocks for over a period of time provides a chance for recovery. A stock can fall down to nil value or zero but has the power to rise infinitely. Hence, holding to stock, even though it under-performs, can pay you well in the long run provided you believe in the vision of the company whose stocks you have held. Investing in the right kind of business is another indispensable attribute that investors have to focus on. Long term stock investment in the right company has the potential to multiply your wealth.

Another benefit that a long-term investor can enjoy is tax advantages on capital gains. Gains achieved by investing in the short term are taxed as regular income. Whereas, profits made by investing for the long term (at least for more than a year) are taxed at rates lower than your income tax bracket. Also, long-term investing helps you to fulfill goals like providing for your child's education, long term funds for your parents, your own personal asset growth goals, or savings for your retirement.

The benefits mentioned above are a few of the common advantages that a long-term investor can enjoy. Investing at the right time, in the right company, and for the right period can make you a good investor.

INVESTING VERSUS GAMBLING

Investing is the act of allocating funds or committing capital to an asset; like stocks, with the expectation of generating an income or profit. The expectation of a return in the form of income or price appreciation is the core premise of investing. Investors must always decide how much money they want to risk. Some traders typically risk 2-5% of their capital base on any particular trade. Longer-term investors continuously hear the virtues of diversification across different asset classes. In essence, this is an investment risk management strategy. Spreading your capital across different assets, or different types of assets within the same class will likely help minimize potential losses. To enhance their holdings' performance, some investors study trading patterns by interpreting stock charts. Stock market technicians try to leverage the charts to glean where the stock is going in the future. This area of study dedicated to analyzing charts is commonly referred to as technical analysis. Investment returns can be affected by the amount of commission an investor must pay a broker to buy or sell stocks on his behalf. When you gamble, you own nothing, but when you invest in a stock, you own a share of the underlying company. Some companies reimburse you for your ownership, in the form of stock dividends.

Gambling is defined as staking something on a contingency. It is also known as betting or wagering. It means risking money on an event that has an uncertain outcome and heavily involves chance. Like investors, gamblers must also carefully weigh the amount of capital they want to put "in play." In some card games, pot odds are a way of assessing your risk capital versus your risk-reward. The amount of money to call a bet compared to what is already in the pot. If the odds are favorable, the player is more likely to "call" the bet. Most professional gamblers are quite proficient at-risk management. They research player or team history, or a horse's bloodlines and track record. Seeking an edge, card players typically look for cues from the other players at the table; great poker players can remember what their opponents wagered twenty (20) hands back. They also study the mannerisms and betting patterns of their opponents with the hope of gaining useful information

In casino gambling, the bettor is playing against "the house." In sports gambling and in lotteries, two of the most common "gambling" activities in which the average person engages bettors are, in a sense betting against each other because the number of players helps determine the odds. In horse racing, for example, placing a bet is a wager against other bettors: The odds on each horse are determined by the amount of money bet on that horse, and constantly change up until the race starts. Generally, the odds are stacked against gamblers. The probability of losing an investment is usually higher than the possibility of winning more than the investment. A gambler's chances of making a profit can also be reduced if they have to put up an additional amount of money beyond their bet, referred to as "points," which is kept by the house whether the bettor wins or loses. Points are comparable to the broker commission or trading fee an investor pays.

Investing vs. Gambling: Key Differences

In both gambling and investing, a fundamental principle is to minimize risk while maximizing profits. But, when it comes to gambling, the house always has an edge a mathematical advantage over the player that increases the longer they play. In contrast, the stock market continually appreciates over the long term. This doesn't mean that a gambler will never hit the jackpot, and it also doesn't mean that a stock investor will always enjoy a positive return. It merely is that over time, if you keep playing, the odds will be in your favor as an investor and not in your favor as a gambler.

Mitigating Loss

Another key difference between investing and gambling is that you have no way to limit your losses. If you pony up $10 a week for the NFL office pool and you don't win, you're out all of your capital. When betting on any pure gambling activity, there are no loss mitigation strategies. In contrast, stock investors and traders have a variety of options to prevent total loss of risked capital. Setting stop losses on your stock investment is a simple way to avoid undue risk. If your stock drops 10% below its purchase price, you have the opportunity to sell that stock to someone else and still retain 90% of your risk capital. However, if you bet $100 that the Jacksonville Jaguars will win the Super Bowl this year, you cannot get part of your money back if they just make it to the Super Bowl. And even if they did win the Super Bowl, don't forget about that point spread: If the team does not win by more points than given by the bettor, the bet is a loss.

The time factor

Another critical difference between the two activities has to do with the concept of time. Gambling is a time-bound event, while an investment in a company can last several years. In gambling, once the game or race or hand is over, your opportunity to profit from your wager has come and gone. You either have won or lost your capital. Stock investing, on the other hand, can be time rewarding. Investors who purchase shares in companies that pay dividends are rewarded for their risked dollars. Companies pay you money regardless of what happens to your risk capital, as long as you hold onto their stock. Savvy investors realize that returns from dividends are a vital component to making money in stocks over the long term.

Getting Information

Both stock investors and gamblers look to the past, studying historical performance and current behavior to improve their chances of making a winning move. Information is a valuable commodity in the world of gambling, as well as stock investing. But there's a difference in the availability of data. Stock and company information is readily available for public use. Company earnings, financial ratios, and management teams can be researched and studied, either directly or via research analyst reports before committing capital. Stock traders who make hundreds of transactions a day can use the day's activities to help with future decisions. In contrast, if you sit down at a blackjack table in Las Vegas, you have no information about what happened an hour, a day, or a week ago at that particular table. You may hear that the table is either hot or cold, but that information is not quantifiable.

RISK AND MONEY MANAGEMENT

Money management is the single most overlooked aspect of trading. It's far more essential to manage your account's value correctly than it is to locate the exact bottom or top of the market. Money management can make the difference between success and failure. If you're considering stock trading and investing, or if your stock market investing strategy isn't as successful as you'd like it to be, you owe it yourself to become an expert at this technique. If you want to make money investing in stocks, you need to be good at money management, not lucky. A lucky streak is always well received, but the moment you require luck to succeed, you'll not make the grade. The key to consistently making money by trading and investing in the stock market is dependent on your knowledge of how to lose money correctly through strict money management techniques. Although this seems opposite to our usual way of thinking, it makes a lot of sense. If you expect to trade and are not willing to accept losses from time to time, it should be understood that this is not a realistic approach. The truth is many of the most successful traders lose money more often than the unsuccessful ones. However, they are still able to achieve success in the long run. In the twenty-first century, it has become fashionable to manage one's investments, yet few traders implement disciplined, professional money management strategies. Professional risk and money

69

management strategies are the foundation for success. Essentially, money management tells you how many shares or contracts to trade at a given point. Money management is a defensive concept. It keeps you in the game to play another day. For example, money management tells you whether you have enough new money to trade additional positions. Don't confuse money management with stop placement. Stop placement does not address how much question. Money management is risk management. Risk management is the difference between success and failure in trading. Trading correctly is 90% money and portfolio management. Unfortunately, this is a fact that most people want to avoid or don't understand. Once you have your money management under control, your discipline and psychology is 100% of your success. Money management optimizes capital usage. Few have the ability to view their portfolios as a whole. Even fewer traders and investors make a move from a defensive or reactive view of risk. They measure risk to avoid losses, to an offensive or proactive posture in which risks are actively managed for more efficient use of capital. Trend following risk management formulas and philosophies are key to increasing profits while controlling risk.

Frequently asked question in Money Management

question: Does money management impact a decision to trade the same number of contracts or shares in all markets?

Answer: Yes. Money and portfolio management rules dictate the number of contracts or shares. Precise formulas set forth size. A trader who uses a constant trading size gives up an important edge in much the same way a blackjack player does when always betting the same regardless of what cards are on the table. Common single contract/share measures of trading system performance such as win/loss ratio, percent winning trades, etc.

They are of little value to decision making when using trend following systems (and the turtle system). Often the best trading approach, when tested on a single contract/share basis, will turn out not to be the best approach when money management strategies are incorporated.

question: What about short term trading? Isn't the short term less risky, and therefore you don't need money management strategies?

Answer: Short term trading is not, by definition, less risky. Some people may mistakenly apply a cause and effect relationship between using a long-term strategy and the potential of incurring a substantial loss. They forget profit and loss are proportional. A short-term system will never allow you to be in the trend long enough to achieve significant profits. You end up with small losses but also small profits. Added together, numerous small losses equal a significant loss. When you trade for the long term, you have a more positive expectation in terms of the size of the move. In the big picture, the larger the move, the larger the validation of the move.

Platforms and tools to use

When choosing an online broker, you'll need to consider these three crucial steps:

- Choose the type of brokerage account you need.
- Consider the features you want and their associated costs.
- Choose the brokerage that best fits your needs.

Step 1: To decide which broker works best for your needs, you first need to think about the different investing styles. Here are common investing styles used today:

- Active management
- Passive management
- Growth investing
- Value investing

Step 2: It's essential to decide which features you will need in a broker. You should consider factors like educational materials, research tools, news access, and how their fees are structured to assess what works best for you. If you are a beginner, it could be best to focus less on their fees and more on what kinds of educational materials they offer. On the other hand, more experienced investors may want advanced charting features and the ability to backtest.

Step 3: Now that you have thought about which investment styles and features are suitable for you, it's time to choose a broker. It's also important to keep in mind that fewer fees and commissions can also mean fewer features, so it's best to research each platform before opening an account.

Tips to follow when choosing an online investment platform

Choosing from a diversity of online investment companies may be a pain in the neck as well as a real breeze. The odds are even. Everything depends on your approach. Either you take the process seriously or let things take their course. Even though you shouldn't invest more than you are ready to lose, it doesn't mean you can just let it slide and pick the first investment platform on the google search results page.

1. Prioritize needs: Before searching for the best investment platforms for beginners on Google, think about your needs and make a list of requirements to a financial website. You may consider achieving your investment goals as the highest priority or seek the most user-friendly portal or want to be serviced as a royal person. Once you've made up your mind, start researching.

2. Research: If you're a first-timer, start with digging into the fundamentals of online brokerage. You may need to understand basic definitions, such as; what is ETF, ISA, and what SIPP stands for. Know the difference between share dealing and currency trading; learn the pros and cons of futures. Run down the list of top investment platforms, they usually provide a brief overview of the specifics of each broker, its pricing policy, benefits, and limitations. However, such ratings are entirely subjective, which doesn't mean that the number one or best-rated broker is your perfect fit. Another option is to scan forums such as quora and Reddit, where people share their successes and less than successful stories. You will eventually bump into one or two investment platforms that suit you best.

3. Vet reputation: For online brokers, impeccable reputation and good reviews are key to success. Almost all websites have areas where people can leave comments describing their attitude to a provider and its services. Also, search for independent reviews written by investment advisors of financial analysts that provide deep insight into all the ins and outs of a company.

4. Compare opportunities and risks: Did you like everything when trying a demo version of your online broker? If yes, then let's compare the investment options you have and the potential risks you can bear. For beginners who have not built a portfolio of preferred assets, new platforms provide enough opportunities; stocks, ETFs, options, and cryptocurrency. Professional investors tend to deal with online brokers offering a wide choice of investment products such as mutual funds, bonds, CFDs, annuities, and forex currency. More options mean a more balanced portfolio, on the one hand, and more commissions and risks of being left with nothing on the other side.

Most of the companies charge a commission between $4.95 and $6.95 on every trade. Some of them, Vanguard, in particular, levy commissions according to an account balance. While others offer bonuses depending on a trading volume, you may pay attention to discounts and bonuses which best online investment sites use to entice traders. But don't forget about exit penalties you must pay in case of leaving a platform.

5. Ask for help: Every financial website offers assistance in everything from how to use a platform to the ways of

building a winning investment strategy. However, the level and quality of help vary. Investors like websites that provide instant support like live chats and callbacks and those who strive to minimize users' efforts in solving different tasks. For instance, 'm1 finance' gives prompts to users on every step in the signup procedure.

Below is a rundown of leading investment supermarkets in the UK and US you may use when doing your research.

- **IGIG**: IGIG is a well-established investment provider based in the UK. The company offers two options; share dealing and IG smart portfolios. The former is for those who prefer DIV investments, and the latter is ideal for clients who seek a hands-off approach. Whatever account you choose, you can opt for an ISA with tax incentives or a SIPP geared towards retirement savings. As for their pricing policy, the share dealing feature is available for £5 if you place 10+ trades a month. For those who are willing to open an ISA or SIPP account or take part in international trading, there are additional fees. IG runs a super cool educational campaign that includes forums, blogs, tutorials, and guidelines, which makes it a good option for beginners.

- **FIDELITY**: Fidelity features one of the best trade routing engines, which results in lower trade costs for their customers. The goal of their trading technology is to achieve price improvement on customer orders. So that "buy" orders are executed at a price lower than the market at the moment the trade is placed, and "sell" orders execute at a higher price. Customers trading quantities over 500 shares can often achieve more price improvement than they pay in commission. Fidelity's portfolio analysis feature lets you link outside accounts, as well as any cryptocurrency you hold at Coinbase, to give you a picture of your overall financial health. Education offerings and tax planning are well integrated, and the site itself is simple to navigate. Their recently redesigned trade ticket reduces the number of clicks needed to place a trade. Fidelity offers a more sophisticated trading site called trade armor for those who want to design an exit plan when opening a new position. The website features screeners for stocks, exchange-traded funds (ETFs), mutual funds, and a variety of fixed income products. Fidelity also received awards for best overall online brokers, best for beginners, best stock trading apps, best for ETFs, best for penny stocks, best for Roth IRAs, best for IRAs and best for international trading.

Pros

- Low commissions tied with excellent education and research.
- Screeners include social responsibility, and themes such as 3d printing, artificial intelligence, founder run firms, and more.
- Banking services offered, including a 2% cashback credit card and atm fee rebates.

- For options traders, a trade ticket has been integrated into the options chain view.
- Portfolio analysis helps customers understand their exposure to sectors, industries, and geographical regions.

Cons

- The website performed erratically during trading surges in the last year.
- No futures trading available.
- Guest access available for 30 days; must deposit funds to maintain access to research, quotes, etc.
- Some features are hard to find due to the deep menu structure of the website.

CHARLES SCHWAB: Schwab customers can take advantage of their ETF one source list, which offers over 200 commission-free exchange-traded funds from 16 different fund families. The ETF screener on the website has nine pre-defined screens, or you can build your own with up to 70 different criteria, including performance, sector, risk measures, and portfolio contents. There are three web-based sites available:

- The standard at schwab.com, plus trade source, which helps customers generate trading ideas.

- The street smart central, which includes advanced options analytics. And

- The live news feed from CNBC.

Trade source's strategy screener lets you choose plain English screens, such as:

"which stocks have been up to or down on a higher than normal percentage of the market's total volume?" Technical analysis from recognia fuels the screener. Charles Schwab also received awards for best overall online brokers, best for international trading, best for options trading, best for penny stocks, best for beginners, best for Roth IRAs, best for IRAs, best for ETFs, and best stock trading apps.

Pros

- Options traders can use the terrific risk analytics built by Options-Xpress; a brokerage Schwab acquired and integrated into their streetsmart edge site.
- The all in one trade ticket lets you build a trade for any asset class you are eligible to utilize, including options, futures, and futures options.
- The idea hub lets you look for trading ideas based on market moves, upcoming earnings announcements, premium harvesting, and covered calls, plus futures options. You can pick a trading idea, run analytics, and then hit the trade button and open a position.

Cons

- There are three web platforms, and you may find yourself switching among them to use all the tools you need.

- The charting functionality in street smart central runs on adobe flash, which causes problems with some operating systems.

- **TD AMERITRADE:** Streaming news and home-grown video is built into the TD Ameritrade website, along with a wealth of education and product offerings. You can read the chatter about your holdings and watch lists using social signals, which pulls information from twitter and organizes tweets for you. You can customize your web experience using TD Ameritrade's dock tool, which lets you include data from other websites such as yahoo. Td Ameritrade also received awards for best overall online brokers, best for day trading, best for options trading, best for beginners, best for ETFs, best for Roth IRAs, best for IRAs and best stock trading apps.

Pros

- Easily defined alerts let you determine what kinds of reports you want, and how frequently you want them delivered.
- Free independent research from a wide variety of sources.
- A trade ticket is displayed at the bottom of every screen so that you can take quick action on your ideas.
- A watch list you set up on your web platform will also display on a mobile app.
- Gains keeper, a capital gains monitor, is free to use.

Cons

- Higher than average commissions and margin rates.
- A glut of features across multiple platforms can make it hard to find the tools you want.
- Multiple options (more than two legs) cannot be traded on the web platform.
- Futures and forex cannot be traded on the web platform.
- **MERRILL EDGE:** Merrill's website offers a lot of help for setting and attaining financial goals. The personal retirement calculator helps you estimate how much you'll need to retire, and then builds an action plan to assist with your wealth building. The portfolio story feature spells out how your assets are allocated by sector and class, and helps you pinpoint underperforming investments to generate higher returns. The advanced web platform, Merrill Edge market pro, features streaming quotes and news along with interactive charting. The market pro dashboard is customizable, allowing you to rearrange the tools to suit your needs. Merrill Edge also received awards for best for beginners, best stock trading apps, best for IRAs, and best for Roth IRAs.

Pros

- Lots of help for planning for goals and assessing your progress.
- Life stage planning gives you specific guidance for your current situation: just starting, building wealth,

nearing retirement, and living in retirement.

- It is extensively integrated with the parent bank of America.
- Those with high balances with Merrill and/or Bank of America can qualify for commission-free stock and ETF trading.

Cons

- Market pro access requires either a high balance or frequent trading activity.
- Frequent prodding to move assets into a managed account, which can cost more.
- No commission-free ETFs available, though customers with high balances with Merrill and/or Bank of America can qualify for 30-100 free stock/ETF trades monthly.
- The waived commissions for premium members cannot be used for options trades.
- **ETRADE**: Etrade's standard web platform includes streaming real-time quotes, news, charts, and daily market commentary. You'll find screeners to help you choose stocks, ETFs, mutual funds, and bonds based on your criteria. Those new to investing can put together customized courses to learn more about selecting and placing trades, and also attend webinars and live events to step up to more sophisticated strategies. Options traders can use screeners and optimizers built by professional market makers on the options house platform. You can close an equity option priced at $0.10 or less for free with the dime buyback program. Advanced

traders can analyze and trade options on futures around the clock. Etrade also received awards for best for options trading, best for ETFs, best stock trading apps, best for Roth Iras, best for Iras, and best for beginners.

Pros

- The options house platform includes videos and calculators to help you learn how and why to trade options.
- The technical insights feature on the options house platform teaches the new technical analyst how to use these studies.
- More than 250 ETFs can be traded commission-free.
- You can get your portfolio up and running quickly with one of Etrade's prebuilt ETF portfolios, all of which use commission-free funds. (minimum $2,500).
- Good tools and flat pricing for bond traders ($1 per bond).

Cons

- Commissions and margin rates are on the high side unless you are a frequent trader.
- You may need to switch back and forth between the Etrade website and the options house platform to take advantage of all the available tools.
- No forex or international trading available.

Parameters to consider when selecting stocks

If you decide that you want to try your hand at stock investing, it's essential to do your homework. You want to choose something that's of good value, especially if you plan to hold on to the stock for a while. As you consider your options, here are some things you should know about a company before you decide to invest:

1. Earnings growth: Check the net gain in income that a company has over time. Look for trends. Does the earnings growth generally increase? Even if the increase isn't dramatic, a company that has steady and consistent earnings growth over time can be a good bet for the future.

2. Stability: Every company is going to have periods where the stock loses value. This is natural, especially during times of economic difficulty and market upheaval. Instead, look for the overall stability as it relates to the economic conditions. Is there a great deal of fluctuation? If so, that could be a red flag. If, however, the company only seems to have real trouble when the rest of the market is struggling, you might do well to consider the stock.

3. Relative strength in the industry: Take a look at the overall company's industry. Does the industry that the stock is in show promise for the future? If so, look closely at the company. What is the company's relative strength in the industry? Is it well placed against its competitors? Take into account the industry as a whole, and the company's place in it.

4. Debt-to-equity ratio: All companies carry debt on the balance sheet. Even the wealthiest companies carry liabilities. However, you want to be careful of companies with high amounts of debt. Look at the company's balance sheet and compare the debt-to-equity ratio. You want a company that has more assets than liabilities. If you want an investment that is likely to present a lower risk, consider a company with a debt-to-equity ratio of 0.30 or below. You can look into companies with higher ratios if you have a little bit higher risk tolerance, or if a higher ratio is acceptable in the industry (construction companies, for example, are known for higher ratios since they use a lot of debt funding).

5. Price-to-earnings ratio: Consider how well the stock's price is doing concerning its earnings. The p/e ratio is often considered one of the most important considerations when it comes to fundamental analysis and value investing. This ratio looks at the company's current price and compares it to the per-share earnings of the company. You figure the p/e ratio as follows: take the current share price and divide it by the earnings per share. So, if a company is trading at $40 per share and the earnings per share are $2.50, the p/e ratio is 16. Understand that the higher the p/e ratio, the greater the expectation that there will be higher growth in the future. While you don't want to rely entirely on this factor, it can help compare a company to others in the same industry.

6. Management: How well is the company managed? Do you feel that those in charge are competent? What is the general culture? Is the company innovative? Also, consider

whether or not a scandal could harm the company. Keep in mind, too, that some scandals only harm the company in the short-term. If the company is likely to recover from the setback, you can get an excellent deal on the share price amid such difficulties.

7. Dividends: A company that pays dividends is often one with a certain amount of stability. However, be careful of companies with very high yields. That can be an indication of coming instability. Additionally, a company that pays a lot in dividends might not be reinvesting in the company. Look for companies that pay modest, but regular (and increasing) dividends over time.

HOW TO DETECT AND AVOID SCAMS

The internet is an excellent tool for investors. It provides a source for researching investments and trading securities with unprecedented ease. Unfortunately, the lack of rules on the web also makes it the perfect place for fraud to flourish. To avoid getting scammed, it is important that you take the necessary precautions.

Below are five ways to reduce your chances of becoming a victim of fraud.

1. Pay attention: Anyone can build a website. There are a variety of tools available online that enable the creation of a basic website with little effort or money. The fact is, the bad guys know how easy it is to build websites, and they also know that many people pay little attention to details when the prospect of easy money is flashed before their eyes. To take advantage of this confluence of events, scam

artists often slap together hastily designed websites, relying on simple math to make a buck. Regardless of how poorly the sites are put together, statistically speaking, it's a number game. A certain number of people will visit a given website, and, out of that number, a smaller number will take the bait.

To screen out the scammers, pay attention to quality when you're surfing the web, especially when money and investments are involved. Typographical errors, content that doesn't make sense, and poor graphic design are signs that a website may not be legitimate. While legitimate sites aren't always perfect, they are usually pretty close. When major financial services firms decided to develop a web presence, a lot of time, talent, and money goes into helping the company put its best face forward. While some scams sites are so detailed that they mirror legitimate sites, paying attention to quality will help you avoid the worst of the rogue sites.

2. Apply common sense: Scam artists understand greed and cater to it by promising to deliver something for nothing. Internet message boards, spam emails, and online investment newsletters are three of the most common tools of the criminal trade. If you think you've found a "golden nugget" on an internet message board, or you have been the lucky recipient of an email from a foreign national desperate to give away millions of dollars in exchange for your help (similar to the Nigerian scam), remember that greed makes you gullible. Sadly, even chief executive officers (CEOS) of major corporations have been caught using assumed names to talk up their companies' stocks and talk down their competitors in online forums. Other fraudsters are even more brazen, intentionally promoting stocks to profit by selling when investors are buying. The proliferation of online investment newsletters touting what is supposed to be "hot" stock picks facilitates this type of fraud. The best way to protect yourself from this type of activity is to apply common sense. No matter what you think you have learned online or how much you have convinced yourself that the information that you have uncovered is legitimate if it looks too good to be true, it probably is.

3. Use the internet: Not everything you read online is false or misleading. All U.S. Companies with more than 500 investors and $10 million assets and all companies listed on major stock exchanges are required to file regular reports with the securities and exchange commission (SEC). While scandals like those at Enron and WorldCom, among many others, have demonstrated that filing these reports doesn't guarantee legitimacy. A quick check of the sec's Edgar website is always a good place to start when researching companies that interest you. At the very least, it verifies the company's existence. While this might sound pretty basic, more than a few scams have made millions of dollars from unsuspecting investors by touting companies that weren't real in addition to the sec's site; there are plenty of sites that track stocks, providing price quotes, corporate news, historical performance data and more. Most of these sites are easy to use and free. For a reasonable fee, there are also plenty of research reports that can be purchased online. These reports are created by reputable financial analysts and provide insight into the operations of the companies they cover.

4. Contact the regulators: If a company that catches your interest shows up in the Edgar database, your next move is to check with your state securities regulator to see if there have been complaints filed against the company. If the company has been touted by a brokerage firm, something that is often seen in newsletters and email, check with your state regulator and with the financial industry regulatory authority (FINRA) to determine whether the brokerage firm has a good disciplinary track record.

5. Conduct fundamental research: If the hot company that you found online has passed all of the other screens, it's time to get serious and do some hands-on research. Get copies of the firm's financial statements and analyze them. Research, the company's leaders. If the company claims to be the largest supplier of widgets to the world's largest grocery store chain, call the store and find out if the claim is true. Make every effort to learn as much about the company as you possibly can. Of course, if all of this sounds like too much work, buy a mutual fund and delegate the work to the professionals.

6. There are no shortcuts: Investing, like any other worthwhile endeavor, requires effort. There are no shortcuts, but there are plenty of pitfalls. The number and types of scams on the internet would take an army of accountants a lifetime to track and calculate, but most are variations on a theme. To minimize your odds of getting scammed, never make an investment decision based strictly on information that you obtained online.

Popular scam

One of the most popular stock schemes is called "pump and dump." Here's how it works. A group of crooks buys up a block of stock in a little-known company, preferably one that has a semi-exciting technology name. They get on the internet and begin flooding cyberspace with false rumors about how this company has some breakthrough technology or just signed a super deal. They may even develop phony letterheads and send out press releases about the company.

In some cases, the company knows nothing about the scheme. It becomes a victim too. In other cases, company insiders execute the scheme. If the crooks are successful, the stock's price will jump as they convince people they are getting in on the ground floor of some big deal. After the stock goes up, the crooks decide when they think it has gone as far as it will go, and then they sell their big block of stock for a fat profit. When they sell, the price drops, and all the people they conned into buying lose money.

START WITH THE SIMULATOR

Stock simulators allow the user to hone their investment techniques. Regardless of your level of proficiency with money management and making investments, dealing with the stock market is still always a bit of a gamble. Before the inception of the internet, old school traders, brokers, and certified public accountants (CPAs) used pen and paper for drawing charts and entering orders. (back in the day, stock market orders were written on paper and then rushed from a brokerage firm's order desk to a floor trader.

Appropriately named stock market "runners" were hired at least partially based on how fast they could run.) The difficulties with traditional paper trading were endless, posing a variety of hazards. One of the most common problems was being unable to read whatever someone scribbled. Another was, at the end of the day, being unable to find all the scraps of paper that documented the day's trading. The advantages offered by high-speed computers, software, the internet, and all its associated technology. One of the major advances and a boon for money managers, brokers, and financial advisors of any type made possible by the development of sophisticated computer programs is the ability to create the best stock simulators or trading simulators for practicing trading techniques and testing out trading strategies.

Using the best stock simulators for practice and strategy trials

A good stock market simulator serves as an excellent practice tool for making investments and trying out trading strategies. Additionally, it offers the opportunity to learn and master finance and investing basics. Simulators can help you learn how to factor in trading costs, sell short, and perform stock analysis. Simulators utilize popular analytical tools such as financial ratios like price/earnings and debt/equity. Simulation trading can also help you perceive how the larger economic picture and business-related news affect markets and stock prices.

Best stock simulators: tools for professionals or individual investors

Anyone who is in the business of serving clients involved in stock market investing wants to take advantage of the best tools available that will help them serve clients better. Individual investors seek out the best stock simulators that will guide them in becoming better investors. The choice of a stock simulator depends mostly on how well a given simulator meets your specific individual needs. There is no one stock market simulator that we would point to and declare as "the best" in all situations. However, the three examined below, are at the very least, "among the best." They have consistently received high marks from both users and reviewers. We urge you to examine them from the perspective of your own specific needs and goals. They are;

1. Wall Street Survivor: Wall Street Survivor is a tried and true stock market simulator. It has been "in the game" for quite a while and qualifies as one of the best stock simulators. It offers a wealth of personal finance and investment knowledge you can absorb at your own speed. While you're practicing and becoming more proficient at trading, you can also effectively earn a graduate degree in investing. You can use Wall Street Survivor to trade your way to the uppermost tier of investors playing the game. As you put into practice the investing skills you've learned, you can earn additional virtual cash, badges of achievement, and prizes that include; ebooks, subscriptions, and even real cash. (So Wall Street Survivor might be the right choice if you need some extra

investment capital.) http://www.wallstreetsurvivor.com/

2. How the market works: This is another veteran entry in the world of stock market simulators. How the market works is near the head of the pack among free simulators tailored for the beginning investor. This simulator is a streaming stock market game played in real-time. It's used by nearly half a million investors, financial professionals, and school classes every year. How the market works, just as its name indicates, is ideal for beginners. It offers all the educational materials and tools needed to obtain a firm, basic understanding of how the stock market works. This simulator isn't only for beginners. It offers sophisticated trading and investing simulations with the ability to practice global trading stocks, ETFs, mutual funds, options, and even commodity futures. As soon as you sign up, you are instantly offered access to thousands of articles, quotes, charts, wall street analyst ratings, news, and financial statements from publicly traded companies. A complete package, how the market works, provides users with tools such as financial calculators, lesson plan rubrics for teachers, and hours of informative and entertaining videos. This simulator is noteworthy because of its suitability for the classroom. It has gained a wide following among educators. The gaming features include the opportunity to create customized, private competitions for individual classes, grades, or other groups. You can design competitions or tailor-made investing scenarios with specific rules such as specific commission rates, trading competition time frames suited to the term of a class, and varied initial cash balances.
Http://www.howthemarketworks.com/

3. Market Watch Virtual Stock Exchange: The Market Watch virtual stock exchange (VSE) game allows users to create a portfolio and trade stocks in real-time. Once you've joined a game, you can discuss strategies with other players. You can also develop your own game for others to join and compete in. You begin by choosing a list of stock symbols to trade in your portfolio and then develop a custom watch list alongside your holdings. When you're ready, turn on advanced features like limit and stop-loss orders. By providing access to interact with other traders, this program offers the opportunity to learn from a variety of skilled traders with diversified backgrounds and trading strategies. In the end, this stock simulator can be an excellent platform to help you build up your investing muscles. Https://www.marketwatch.com/game

In conclusion, trading stock markets is a tricky business, and there is rarely a single investor beginner or otherwise who becomes hugely successful right out of the gate. It's a simple fact that, as is the case with learning and developing any new skill, practicing at stock trading can become a very valuable aid in becoming a super-successful investor. Using a stock market simulator allows you to practice the art of trading while you're learning the game of investing. It is ideally helping you ultimately to become a more skilled and successful investor in real life.

INVESTING STRATEGIES

OPTION TRADING

Option(s) trading is simply trading options. It is typically done with securities on the stock or bond market (as well as ETFs and the likes). For starters, you can only buy or sell options through a brokerage like ETrade (ETFC) or Fidelity (FNF). When buying a call option, the strike price of an option for a stock, for example, will be determined based on the current price of that stock. For example, if a share of a given stock (like Amazon (AMZN)) is $1,748, any strike price (the price of the call option) that is above that share price is considered to be "out of the money.

"Conversely, if the strike price is under the current share price of the stock, it's considered "in the money." However, for put options (right to sell), the opposite is true with strike prices below the current share price being considered "out of the money" and vice versa. More importantly, any "out of the money" options (whether call or put options) are worthless at expiration (so you want to have an "in the money" option when trading on the stock market).

Another way to think of it is that call options are generally bullish, while put options are generally bearish. Options typically expire on Fridays with different time frames (for example, monthly, bi-monthly, quarterly, etc.). It is, however, important to note that many options contracts are six months.

Primary uses of options

Investors use options for two primary reasons; to speculate and also hedge risks. Every time you buy a stock, you are essentially speculating on the direction the stock will move. Wall Street has coined the phrase "investing" so that buying stock does not sound so risky. But the truth is that we are always uncertain about which direction any equity investor is going to go. You might say that you are positive that IBM is heading higher as you buy the stock, and indeed more often than not, you may even be right.

However, if you were positive that IBM was going to head sharply higher, then you would invest everything you had into buying the stock. All rational investors realize that there is no "sure thing" when it comes to investing, as every investment incurs at least some risk. This risk is what the investor is compensated for when he or she purchases an asset. When you purchase options as a means to speculate on future stock price movements, you are limiting your downside risk, yet your upside earnings potential is unlimited.

Aside from speculations, investors also use options for hedging purposes. A hedge is not just a little green bush in your front yard; it is a way to protect your portfolio from disaster. Hedging is like buying insurance. You buy it as a means of protection against unforeseen events, but you hope you never have to use it. The fact that you hold insurance helps you sleep better at night. Consider this, majority buys homeowners insurance, but why exactly do they do this? Since the odds of having your house destroyed are relatively small, this may seem like a foolish investment to make. After all, most of us will never have a fire, flood, or any other hazard that would cause us to cash in on our insurance. However, we all continue to pay our insurance premiums every year.

Why do we go on paying these hefty fees year after year instead of spending the money on something we would perhaps enjoy more? The answer to this question is obvious. Homes are precious to us, and we would be devastated by their loss. As a way of handling the fear of loss, no matter how remote the chances of loss might be, most of us will happily pay someone else every year to bear this risk for us. When you employ specific options strategies as a means to hedge your portfolio, you are essentially doing the same thing. That is, paying someone to protect you from unforeseen risks.

What are the options?

An option is a contract that allows (but doesn't require) an investor to buy or sell an underlying instrument like a security, ETF, or even index at a predetermined price over a certain period. Buying and selling options are done on the options market, which trades contracts based on securities. Buying an option that allows you buy shares at a later time is called a "call option," whereas buying an option that allows you to sell shares at a later time is called a "put option." However, options are not the same thing as stocks because they do not represent ownership in a company. Although futures use contracts just like options do, options are considered lower risk because you can withdraw (or walk away from) an options contract at any point. The price of the option (it's premium) is thus a percentage of the underlying asset or security.

When buying or selling options, the investor or trader has the right to exercise that option at any point up until the expiration date. Put, buying, or selling an option doesn't mean you have to exercise it at the buy/sell point. As a result of this system, options are considered derivative securities. This means their price is derived from something else (in this case, from the value of assets like the market, securities, or other underlying instruments). For this reason, options are often considered less risky than stocks (if used correctly). But why would an investor use options? Buying options is basically betting on stocks to go up, down, or to hedge a trading position in the market. The price at which you agree to buy the underlying security through the option is called the "strike price," and the fee you pay for buying that option contract is called the "premium." When determining the strike price, you are betting that the asset (typically a stock) will go up or down in price. The price you are paying for that bet is the premium, which is a percentage of the value of that asset.

There are two different kinds of options: 'Call and Put options', which give the investor the right (but not obligation) to sell or buy securities.

CALL OPTIONS

A call option is a contract that gives the investor the right to buy a certain amount of shares (typically 100 per contract) of a particular security or commodity at a specified price over a certain period. For example, a call option would allow a trader to buy a certain amount of shares of either stock, bonds, or even other instruments like ETFs or indexes at a future time (by the expiration of the contract). If you're buying a call option, it means you want the stock (or other security) to go up in price so that you can make a profit off of your contract by exercising your right to buy those stocks (and usually immediately sell them to cash in on the profit). The fee you are paying to buy the call option is called the premium (it's essentially the cost of buying the contract, which will allow you to buy the stock or security eventually). In this sense, the premium of the call option is sort of like a down payment like you would place on a house or car. When purchasing a call option, you agree with the seller on a strike price and are given the option to buy the security at a predetermined price (which doesn't change until the contract expires). So, call options are also much like insurance. You are paying for a contract that expires at a set time but allows you to purchase a security (like a stock) at a predetermined price (which won't go up even if the price of the stock in the market does). However, you will have to renew your option (typically on a weekly, monthly, or quarterly basis).

For this reason, options are always experiencing what's called time decay. This means their value decays over time. For call options, the lower the strike price, the more intrinsic value the call option has.

PUT OPTIONS

A put option is a contract that gives the investor the right to sell a certain amount of shares (again, typically 100 per contract) of a certain security or commodity at a specified price over a certain period. Like call options, a put option allows the trader the right (but not obligation) to sell a security by the contract's expiration date. Like call options, the price at which you agree to sell the stock is called the strike price, and the premium is the fee you are paying for the put option. Put options operate in a similar fashion to call options, except you want the security to drop in price if you are buying a put option in order to make a profit (or sell the put option if you think the price will go up). On the contrary to call options, with put options, the higher the strike price, the more intrinsic value the put option has.

Options Trading Strategies

When trading options, the contracts will typically take this form: Stock ticker (name of the stock), date of expiration (typically in mm/dd/yyyy, although sometimes dates are flipped with the year first, month second and day last), the strike price, call or put, and the premium price (for example, $3). So an example of a call option for Apple stock would look something like this: APPL 01/15/2018 200 Call @ 3.

Still, depending on what platform you are trading on, the option trade will look very different. There are numerous strategies you can employ when options trading, all of which vary in risk, reward, and other factors. And while there are dozens of strategies (most of them fairly complicated), here are a few main strategies that have been recommended for beginners.

1. Straddles and strangles: Using straddles, a trader expects the asset (like a stock) to be highly volatile, but doesn't know the direction in which it will go (up or down). When using a straddle strategy, the trader buys a call and put option at the same strike price, underlying price, and expiry date. This strategy is often used when a trader is expecting the stock of a particular company to plummet or skyrocket, usually following an event like an earnings report. For example, when a company like Apple (AAPL) is getting ready to release their third quarter earnings on July 31st, an options trader could use a straddle strategy to buy a call option to expire on that date at the current Apple stock price. And also buy a put option to expire on the same day for the same price. For strangles (long in this example), an investor will buy an "out of the money" call and an "out of the money" put simultaneously for the same expiry date for the same underlying asset. Investors who use this strategy are assuming the underlying asset (like a stock) will have a dramatic price movement but don't know in which direction. What makes a long strangle a somewhat safe trade is that the investor only needs the stock to move greater than the total premium paid, but it doesn't matter in which direction. The upside of a strangle strategy is that; there is less risk of loss since the premiums are less expensive due to how the options are "out of

the money," which means they are cheaper to buy.

2. Covered Call: If you have long asset investments (like stocks, for example), a covered call is a great option for you. This strategy is typically good for investors who are only neutral or slightly bullish on a stock. A covered call works by buying 100 shares of regular stock and selling one call option per 100 shares of that stock. This kind of strategy can help reduce the risk of your current stock investments but also provides you an opportunity to make a profit with the option. Covered calls can earn you money when the stock price increases or stays pretty constant over the time of the option contract. However, you could lose money with this kind of trade if the stock price falls too much (but can actually still make money if it only falls a little bit). But by using this strategy, you are actually protecting your investment from decreases in share price while allowing yourself to make money while the stock price is flat.

3. Selling Iron Condors: Using this strategy, the trader's risk can either be conservative or risky depending on their preference (which is a definite plus). For iron condors, the position of the trade is non-directional, which means the asset (like a stock) can either go up or down. This means there is profit potential for a reasonably wide range. To use this kind of

strategy, sell a put and buy another put at a lower strike price (essentially, a put spread), and combine it by buying a call and selling a call at a higher strike price (a call spread). These calls and puts are short. When the stock price stays between the two puts or calls, you make a profit (so, when the price fluctuates somewhat, you're making money). But the strategy loses money when the stock price either increases drastically above or drops drastically below the spreads. For this reason, the iron condor is considered a neutral market position.

SWING TRADE EXPLAINED

Swing trading is a style of trading that attempts to capture gains in a stock or any financial instrument over a period ranging from a few days to several weeks. Swing traders primarily use technical analysis to look for trading opportunities. These traders may utilize fundamental analysis in addition to analyzing price trends and patterns.

The goal of swing trading is to capture a chunk of a potential price move. While some traders seek out volatile stocks with lots of movement, others may prefer more sedate stocks. In either case, swing trading is the process of identifying where an asset's price is likely to move next, entering a position, and then capturing a chunk of the profit from that move. Successful swing traders are only looking to capture a chunk of the expected price move, and then move on to the next opportunity.

Points to note

1. Swing trading involves taking trades that last a couple of days up to several months to profit from an anticipated price move.
2. Swing trading exposes a trader to overnight and weekend risk, where the price could gap and open the following session at a substantially different price.
3. Swing traders can take profits utilizing an established risk/reward ratio based on a stop loss and profit target, or they can take profits or losses based on a technical indicator or price action movements.
4. Swing trading is one of the most popular forms of active trading, where traders look for intermediate-term opportunities using various types of technical analysis.

Many swing traders assess trades on a risk/reward basis. By analyzing the chart of an asset, they determine where they will enter, where they will place a stop loss, and then anticipate where they can get out with a profit. If they are risking $1 per share on a setup that could reasonably produce a $3 gain, that is a favorable risk/reward. On the other hand, risking $1 to make $1 or only make $0.75 isn't as favorable.

Swing traders primarily use technical analysis due to the short term nature of the trades. Fundamental analysis can also be used to enhance the analysis. For example, if a swing trader sees a bullish setup in stock, they may want to verify that the fundamentals of the asset looks favorable or are also improving. Swing traders will often look for opportunities on the daily charts and may watch 1-hour or 15-minute charts to find precise entry and stop-loss points.

Advantages

1. It requires less time to trade than day trading.
2. Maximizes short-term profit potential by capturing the bulk of market swings.
3. Traders can rely exclusively on technical analysis, simplifying the trading process.

Disadvantages

1. Trade positions are subject to overnight and weekend market risk.
2. Abrupt market reversals can result in substantial losses.
3. Swing traders often miss longer term trends in favor of short term market moves.

Swing Trading Strategy

A swing trader tends to look for multi-day chart patterns. Some of the more common patterns involve moving average crossovers, cup and handle patterns, head and shoulders patterns, flags, and triangles. Key reversal candlesticks may be used in addition to other indicators to devise a solid trading plan. Ultimately, each swing trader devises a plan and strategy that gives them an edge over many trades. This involves looking for trade setups that tend to lead to predictable movements in the asset's price.

This isn't easy, and no strategy or setup works every time. With a favorable risk/reward, winning every time isn't required. The more convenient the risk/reward of a trading strategy, the fewer times it needs to win to produce an overall profit over many trades.

Example: Other than targeting 20% to 25% profits for most of your stocks, the profit goal is a more modest 10%, or even just 5% in tougher markets. Those types of gains might not seem to be the life-changing rewards typically sought in the stock market, but this is where the time factor comes in. The swing trader's focus isn't on gains developing over weeks or months; the average length of trade is more like 5 to 10 days. In this way, you can make a lot of small wins, which will add up to significant overall returns. If you are happy with a 20% gain over a month or more, 5% to 10% gains every week or two can add up to significant profits. Swing trading can still deliver larger gains on individual trades. A stock may exhibit enough initial strength that it can be held for a bigger gain, or partial profits can be taken while giving the remaining position room to run.

Swing trade bonus strategy for a long term investment

Below are some rules for investors using Swing Trade:

1. Always align your trade with the overall direction of the market.

2. Go long, strength. Go short, weakness.

3. Always trade in harmony with the trend one-time frame

above the one you are trading.

4. Never trade only on the short-term chart of the swing-trading time frame.

5. Try to enter the trade near the beginning of the trend, not near the end.

6. Always apply the rule of "multiple indicators." Do not trade on any one technical tool or concept in isolation.

7. Keep your eye on the ball. Track a consistent group of stocks.

8. Always enter a trade with a clear trading plan, the four key elements of which are a target, a limit, a stop loss, and an add-on point.

9. Try to put the odds in your favor.

10. Be a "techno-fundamentalist" and integrate fundamentals into your technical analysis.

11. Master the "inner game" of swing trading. Great trading is psychological as well as technical.

EXCHANGE TRADED FUND

An exchange traded fund (ETF) is an investment fund traded on stock exchanges, much like stocks. An ETF holds assets such as stocks, commodities, or bonds and generally operates with an arbitrage mechanism designed to keep it trading close to its net asset value, although deviations can occasionally occur. Most ETFs track an index, such as a stock index or bond index. ETFs may be attractive as investments because of their low costs, tax efficiency, and stock-like features. ETF distributors only buy or sell ETFs directly from or to authorized participants. These participants are large broker dealers with whom they have entered into agreements and then, only in creation units, which are large blocks of tens of thousands of ETF shares, usually exchanged in kind with baskets of the underlying securities. Authorized participants may wish to invest in the ETF shares for the long term, but they usually act as market makers on the open market. Using their ability to exchange creation units with their underlying securities to provide liquidity of the ETF shares and help ensure that their intraday market price approximates the net asset value of the underlying assets.

Other investors, such as individuals using a retail broker trade ETF shares on this secondary market. An ETF combines the valuation feature of a mutual fund or unit investment trust, which can be bought or sold at the end of each trading day for its net asset value with the tradability feature of a closed-end fund; which trades throughout the trading day at prices that may be more or less than its net asset value. Closed-end funds are not considered to be ETFs, even though they are funds and are traded on an exchange. ETFs have been available in the US since 1993 and in Europe since 1999. ETFs traditionally have been index funds, but in 2008 the U.S. Securities and Exchange Commission began to authorize the creation of actively managed ETFs. ETFs offer both tax efficiency as well as lower transaction and management costs. More than \$2 trillion were invested in ETFs in the United States between when they were introduced in 1993 and 2015. By the end of 2015, ETFs offered "1,800 different products, covering almost every conceivable market sector, niche, and trading strategy".

PRO OF ETFS

Since their introduction in 1993, exchange-traded funds (ETFs) have exploded in popularity, with investors looking for alternatives to mutual funds. Both institutions and individuals could see the benefit of these instruments as a basket of assets designed to track an index that offered low management fees and higher intraday price visibility. But of course, no investment is perfect, and ETFs have their downsides (low dividends, large bid-ask spreads) too. Identifying the advantages and disadvantages of ETFs can help investors navigate the risks and rewards, and decide whether these securities, now a quarter century old, make sense for their portfolios.

There are numerous advantages to ETFs, some include;

- Diversification: One ETF can give exposure to a group of equities, market segments, or styles. An ETF can track a broader range of stocks, or even attempt to mimic the returns of a country or a group of countries.
- Trades like a Stock: Although the ETF might give the holder the benefits of diversification, it has the trading liquidity of equity.
- ETFs can be purchased on margin and sold short. ETFs trade at a price that is updated throughout the day. An open-ended mutual fund, on the other hand, is priced at the end of the day at the net asset value.
- ETFs also allow you to manage risk by trading futures and options like stocks. ETFs trade like stocks, as such, you can quickly look up the approximate daily price change using its ticker symbol and compare it to its indexed sector or commodity. Many stock websites also have better interfaces for manipulating charts than commodity websites, and even provide applications for your mobile devices.
- Lower Fees: ETFs, which are passively managed, have much lower expense ratios compared to actively managed funds. What drives up a mutual fund's expense ratio? Costs such as a management fee, shareholder accounting expenses at the fund level, service fees like marketing, paying a board of directors, and load fees for sale and distribution.
- Immediately Reinvested Dividends: The dividends of the companies in an open-ended ETF are

reinvested immediately, whereas, the exact timing for reinvestment can vary for index mutual funds. (One exception, dividends in unit investment trust ETFs are not automatically reinvested, thus creating a dividend drag.)

- Limited Capital Gains Tax: ETFs can be more tax-efficient than mutual funds. As passively managed portfolios, ETFs (and index funds) tend to realize fewer capital gains than actively managed mutual funds. Also, when an ETF buys or sells shares, it's considered an in-kind redemption and does not result in a tax charge. Mutual funds, on the other hand, are required to distribute capital gains to shareholders if the manager sells securities for a profit. This distribution amount is made according to the proportion of the holders' investment and is taxable. If other mutual fund holders sell before the date of record, the remaining holders divide up the capital gain and thus pay taxes even if the fund overall went down in value.

- Lower Discount or Premium in Price: There is a lower chance of ETF share prices being higher or lower than their actual value. ETF's trade throughout the day at a price close to the price of the underlying securities, so if the price is significantly higher or lower than the net asset value, arbitrage will bring the price back in line. Unlike closed-end index funds, ETFs trade based on supply and demand, and market makers will capture price discrepancy profits.

EXCHANGE TRADED FUND AND DIVIDENS

Although exchange-traded funds (ETFs) are primarily associated with index tracking and growth investing, many offer income by owning dividend-paying stocks. When they do, they collect the regular dividend payments and then distribute them to the ETF shareholders. These dividends can be distributed in two ways, at the discretion of the fund's management; cash paid to the investors or reinvestments into the ETFs' underlying investments.

The timing of ETF dividend payments

Similar to an individual company's stock, an ETF sets an ex-dividend date, a record date, and a payment date. These dates determine who receives the dividend and when the dividend gets paid. The timing of these dividend payments are on a different schedule than those of the underlying stocks and vary depending on the ETF. For example, the ex-dividend date for the popular SPDR S&P 500 ETF (SPY) is the third Friday of the final month of a fiscal quarter (March, June, September, and December). If that day happens not to be a business day, then the ex-dividend date falls on the prior business day. The record date comes two days before the ex-dividend date. At the end of each quarter, the SPDR S&P 500 ETF distributes the dividends. Each ETF sets the timing for its dividend dates. These dates are listed in the funds' prospectus, which is publicly available to all investors. Like any company's shares, the price of an ETF often rises before the ex-dividend date, reflecting a flurry of buying activity and falls afterward. As a result, investors who own the fund before the ex-dividend date receive the dividend, while buying afterward do not.

Dividends paid in cash

The SPDR S&P 500 ETF pays out dividends in cash. According to the fund's prospectus, the SPDR S&P 500 ETF puts all dividends it receives from its underlying stock holdings into a non-interest bearing account; until it is time to make a payout. At the end of the fiscal quarter, when dividends are due to be paid, the SPDR S&P 500 ETF pulls the dividends from the non-interest bearing account and distributes them proportionally to the investors. Some other ETFs may temporarily reinvest the dividends from the underlying stocks into the holdings of the fund until it is time to make a cash dividend payment. Naturally, this creates a small amount of leverage in the fund, which can slightly improve its performance during bull markets and slightly harm its performance during bear markets.

Dividends Reinvested

ETF managers may also have the option of reinvesting their investors' dividends into the ETF rather than distributing them as cash. The payout to the shareholders can also be accomplished through reinvestment in the ETFs underlying index on their behalf. Essentially, it comes out the same. For example; If an ETF shareholder receives a 2% dividend reinvestment from an ETF, he may turn and sell those shares if he'd rather have the cash. Sometimes these reinvestments can be seen as a benefit, as it does not cost the investor a trade fee to purchase the additional shares through the dividend reinvestment. However, each shareholder's annual dividends are taxable in the year they are received, even if they are received via dividend reinvestment.

Taxes on dividends in ETFs

Exchange Traded Funds are often viewed as a favorable alternative to mutual funds in terms of their ability to control the amount and timing of income tax to the investor. However, this is primarily due to how and when the taxable capital gains are captured in ETFs. It is important to understand that owning dividend-producing ETFs does not defer the income tax created by the dividends paid by an ETF during a tax year. The dividends that an ETF pays are taxable to the investor in essentially the same way as the dividends paid by a mutual fund.

EXCHANGE TRADED FUND MAKE EASY

ETFs generally provide easy diversification, low expense ratios, and tax efficiency of index funds, while still maintaining all the features of ordinary stock. These features include; limit orders, short selling, and options. ETFs can be economically acquired, held, and disposed of. As such, some investors invest in ETF shares as a long-term investment for asset allocation purposes. Other investors trade ETF shares frequently to hedge risk over short periods or implement market timing investment strategies.

Some of the advantages of ETFs are:

- Lower costs: ETFs generally have lower costs than other investment products because most ETFs are not actively managed. Also, ETFs are insulated from the costs of having to buy and sell securities to accommodate shareholder purchases and redemptions.

ETFs typically have lower marketing, distribution, and accounting expenses.

- Buying and selling flexibility: ETFs can be bought and sold at current market prices at any time during the trading day. Unlike mutual funds and unit investment trusts, which can only be traded at the end of the trading day. As publicly traded securities, their shares can be purchased on margin and sold short, enabling the use of hedging strategies, and traded using stop orders and limit orders. That allows investors to specify the price points at which they are willing to trade.

- Tax efficiency: ETFs generally generate relatively low capital gains. This is because they typically have a low turnover of their portfolio securities. While this is an advantage they share with other index funds, their tax efficiency is further enhanced because they do not have to sell securities to meet investor redemptions.

- Market exposure and diversification: ETFs provide an economical way to rebalance portfolio allocations and to "equitize" cash by investing it quickly. An index ETF inherently provides diversification across an entire index. ETFs offer exposure to a diverse variety of markets, including broad-based indices, broad-based international and country-specific indices, industry sector-specific indices, bond indices, and commodities.

- Transparency: ETFs, whether index funds or actively managed, have transparent portfolios and are priced at frequent intervals throughout the trading day. It is, however, important to note that some of these advantages derive from the status of most ETFs as index funds.

DOLLAR COST AVERAGING STRATEGY

Dollar-cost averaging is the strategy of spreading out your stock or fund purchases, buying at regular intervals, and in roughly equal amounts. When done properly, it can have significant benefits for your portfolio. This is because dollar-cost averaging "smoothen" your purchase price over time and helps ensure that you're not dumping all your money in at a high point for prices. Dollar-cost averaging can be especially powerful in a bear market. It allows you to "buy the dips" or purchase stock at low points when most investors are too afraid to buy. Committing to this strategy means that you will be investing when the market or a stock is down, and that's when investors score the best deals.

Benefits of dollar-cost averaging

Dollar-cost averaging provides three key benefits that can result in better returns. It can help you:

- Avoid mistiming the market
- Take the emotion out of investing
- Think longer-term

In other words, dollar cost averaging saves investors from their psychological biases. Sometimes, investors swing between fear and greed. They are prone to making emotional trading decisions as the market gyrates. However, if you're dollar-cost averaging, you'll be buying when people are selling fearfully, scoring a nice price, and setting yourself up for strong long-term gains. The market tends to go up over time, and dollar-cost averaging can

115

help you recognize that a bear market is a great long-term opportunity rather than a threat.

Drawbacks of dollar-cost averaging

The two downsides of dollar-cost averaging are modest. First, buying more frequently adds to trading costs. However, with brokerages charging ever less to trade, this expense becomes more manageable. Moreover, if you're investing longer-term, fees should become very small relative to your overall portfolio. You're buying for the long haul, not trading in and out of the market. Second, by dollar-cost averaging, you may forgo gains that you otherwise would have earned if you had invested in a lump-sum purchase, and the stock rises. However, the success of that large purchase relies on timing the market correctly, and investors are notoriously terrible at predicting short-term movement of a stock or the market. If a stock does move lower in the near term, dollar-cost averaging means you should come out way ahead of a lump-sum purchase if the stock moves back up.

How to start dollar-cost averaging

You can make dollar-cost averaging as easy as investing in your 401(k) with a little legwork upfront. In fact, you may already be dollar-cost averaging if you're regularly contributing to a 401(k) at your workplace. Setting up a plan with most brokerages isn't hard, though you'll have to select which stock or ideally, which well-diversified exchange-traded fund you'll purchase. Then you can instruct your brokerage to set up a plan to buy automatically at regular intervals. Even if your brokerage account doesn't offer an automatic trading plan, you can set up your purchases on a fixed schedule. For example; the first Monday of the month. You can suspend the investments if you need to, though the point here is to keep investing regularly, regardless of stock prices and market anxieties. Remember, bear markets are an opportunity when it comes to dollar-cost averaging.

Here's one final trick to add a little extra juice to dollar-cost averaging, many stocks and funds pay dividends. And you can often instruct a brokerage to reinvest those dividends automatically. That helps you continue to buy the stock and compound your gains over time.

COMMON MISTAKES TO AVOID IN EXCHANGE TRADED FUND (ETF)

The keys to successfully manage a portfolio include diversification and patience. When considering your ETF purchases, be sure to avoid these common mistakes that investors make:

- Improper Diversification: Not putting all your eggs in one basket is perhaps the first commandment of investing, but it is astonishing how many sinners there are among us. ETFs allow for easy and effective diversification. By investing in ETFs rather than individual securities, you have already taken a step in the right direction. Don't blow it by pouring all your money into one ETF in a single hot sector. You want to invest in both stock and bond ETFs, and both U.S. and international securities. You want diversification on all sides. Invest, to the extent possible, mostly in broad markets: value, growth, small-cap, and large-cap. On the international side of your portfolio, you aim to invest more in regions than in individual countries. ETFs make such diversification easy. Keep in mind that if you invest in stock ETFs, that scenario is going to happen. It has happened many times in the past; it will happen many times in the future. That's just the nature of the beast. If you sell when the going gets tough, you lose the game. The stock market is resilient.

- Too much attention to recent performance: Many investors make a habit of bailing out of whatever market segment has recently dived. Conversely, they often look for whatever market segment has recently shot through the roof, and that's the one they buy. Then, when that market segment tanks, they sell once again. By forever buying high and selling low, their portfolios dwindle over time to nothing. When you build your portfolio, don't overload it with last year's ETF superstars. You don't know what will happen next year.

Below are some of the biggest behavioral mistakes investors make with mutual funds:

- Being overconfident in your ability to predict future investment performance of markets and fund managers: This involves hanging on to a mediocre mutual fund in the hope of eventually getting "even." Being too myopic about the inevitable

118

short term losses accompanying stock ownership and being oblivious to the corrosive impact of compounding costs on long-term returns. A closer look at these mistakes and the impact they will have on your performance can help you identify your susceptibility to error.

- Overconfidence: Some persons are typically are overconfident. For instance, research indicates that people overestimate their abilities as drivers. Also, it's common for a person to think of himself as being above average. Gender also matters to an extent. Men tend to exhibit more overconfidence than women. Overconfidence also applies to invest acumen. Individuals feel confident in their abilities to pick sectors, superstar fund managers, or to time the market properly. Fund managers themselves often are overconfident of their skill to pick winning stocks and sectors and to time the market. A moderate amount of overconfidence is beneficial in many areas of life. People who have confidence tend to be happier and work harder. They also can better cope with life's uncertainties. Unfortunately, being overconfident about investments is dangerous because the stock market is highly effective at deflating overblown egos. Most people don't realize how difficult it is to beat, let alone match the S&P 500's long-term average return of about 10% annually. Overconfidence often leads to overtrading. Investors' fund trading proclivities are evident from the tens of millions of exchange-traded fund shares changing hands daily. A person might be buying and selling actively managed mutual funds to find the next Peter Lynch. The widely popular discount brokerage trading arenas allow impulsive individuals to jump from one fund family to the next with a quick phone call or a few mouse clicks. The overconfident investor may also make big bets by concentrating on a favorite fund or even margining a position.

Ignoring Costs Over Time: People, particularly those who are not finance experts, often treat small numbers as unimportant. Their bias toward big numbers may cause them to focus on those funds that generated the highest returns during the past year. These same people will also ignore what may seem to be minor differences in small numbers, such as expense ratios. The reported net return earned on a fund equals its gross return minus its costs. Expense ratios of mutual funds range from less than 0.20% for low-cost index funds to more than 2%. Assume a $10,000 initial investment and a 10% return. An actively managed large-cap domestic equity fund with a 1.25% expense ratio consumes $895 (or 5.55%) of the $16,105 future gross wealth in five years.

In contrast, over 40 years, the fund's $166,062 in costs devours 36.69% of the $452,593 gross wealth. (Stated differently, only 63.31% of the gross return remains.) The expense drag is far less with a broad-based domestic equity index fund. With a 0.20% expense ratio, the latter would cost an investor $31,775 in 40 years, a modest 7.02% of the future index value. Thus, the fund earns 92.98% of the return of the zero-cost index. Even lower expense ratios can be found on the lowest-cost index funds and the broad-based exchange-traded funds. The expense ratio is not the only cost mutual fund investors face. Even some index funds impose front-end loads these days.

CONCLUSION

The stock market is not a playground. It is neither a bed of roses as even the best traders and investors have, at some point, suffered some loss. As a beginner, investing in the stock market could be difficult. Nevertheless, whether or not you would amass wealth or drown in the pool of losses depends on the path you choose to tread. A wise investor does his homework. He/She understands the value of information as well as the need to acquire knowledge about fundamental aspects such as stocks, the market, the company, behavioral patterns, successful traders, and investors, among several others.

Furthermore, by taking this course, you have taken a step on the journey to becoming a successful trader and investor. However, it is by applying and adhering to some (the ones that best work for you) of the guidelines, principles, strategies, and lessons as explained in the course, that you will eventually achieve your desired feet. A wise investor understands that knowledge is infinite. As such, irrespective of what he knows at the moment, he is always on the lookout for more.